HERE I AM
the Sojourner's bible

10MileMark
www.10MileMark.com

Here I Am Copyright © 2025 10MileMark

All rights reserved. No part of this book may be reproduced in any form or by any electronic or mechanical means, including information storage and retrieval systems, without written permission from the author, except in the case of a reviewer, who may quote brief passages embodied in critical articles or in a review.

This is a work of fiction. Names, characters, places, and incidents either are the product of the author's imagination or are used fictitiously, and any resemblance to actual persons, living or dead, events, or locales is entirely coincidental.

Published by 10MileMark

ISBN: 979-8-218-72508-2

Dedication

To everyone who has touched my life and to the guy who drove 95 mph on a busy street to get to the hospital

Acknowledgments

The departed Dr. John Flowers who opened my eyes many years ago to wisdom, philosophy, and humility

Contents

Acknowledgments............................ i
1 The Book of Sojourners................. 1
2 The Book of Mystery...................... 9
3 The Book of Stewards.................. 23
4 The Book of Expectations............33
5 The Book of Paths........................45
6 The Book of Wonder.................... 55
7 The Book of Limits....................... 69
8 The Book of Tides........................ 83
9 The Book of Seasons.................... 93
10 The Book of Work...................... 107
11 The Book of Emptiness............. 119
12 The Book of Predispositions..... 135
13 The Book of Voices.................... 145
14 The Book of Choices.................. 159
15 The Book of Perspectives.......... 171
16 The Book of Shadows................ 181
17 The Book of Freedom................197
18 The Book of Failure................... 209
19 The Book of Celebration........... 223
20 The Book of Legacy................... 235
21 The Book of Yesterday............... 247
22 The Book of Healing.................. 257
23 The Book of Beginnings............ 265
24 The Book of Waiting.................. 281
25 The Book of Tomorrow............. 293
26 The Book of Surrender.............. 305
Epilogue.. 315

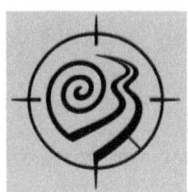

1

the Book of Sojourners

1 Moments define us. Moments make us. They shape and change us. Moments are the markers of time on our journey.

2 As the wisdom of our age declares, "Life is not measured by the number of breaths we take, but by the moments that take our breath away."

3 The truth is we merely pass through time, but we live in moments. We may forget times, but we remember the moments.

4 Moments are the birthplace of memories. Memories are seeds of our emotions and thoughts.

5 When a moment arises, in that moment you can create a landmark on your path, or a regret along your way. It is a

moment in which you can find yourself, become yourself, be yourself.

6 Memory is made when you are totally immersed, all senses engaged, in the moment. It can be a moment of clarity about life and your place in it, revealing what is most important in your temporary dwelling here.

7 And then there are the moments that divide our journey into "before" and "after" - moments when our transient nature suddenly becomes not an abstract concept but a vivid reality.

2 Ancient wise ones saw two kinds of time: chronos time—the regular passing of hours and days—and kairos time: those special moments of opportunity when everything changes on our path.

2 Suddenly realizing we won't live forever is the ultimate kairos moment, the moment when we realize that moments are not guaranteed, a break in how we experience time that forever divides our journey into two separate chapters.

3 This awareness can come in many ways: seeing someone die, nearly dying ourselves, or simply having a moment when we see through the illusion that we'll be here forever.

4 What came before—daily worries, casual plans for tomorrow, the unconscious belief that we're here to stay—suddenly feels like it belonged to someone else's life.

5 What comes after is a new reality—knowing that our stay is short, our time limited, our journey has an end.

6 In that moment, we feel a split in our "lived body"—that seamless connection between our physical self and our conscious experience that we usually take for granted.

7 Suddenly, your body isn't just how you move through life but a temporary home with its own timeline.

8 You look at others—people building permanent structures, both physical and symbolic—and feel confused that

they can live as though they'll stay forever when you now know they won't.

9 The world keeps going as usual, but you're suddenly moving through it with new eyes.

10 We are sojourners, not permanent residents, in this life.

3 This split between life before and after marks a deep change in how we see ourselves. Our understanding of our journey changes completely.

2 How we see our place in this world, how we fit among our fellow sojourners, suddenly needs to be rebuilt.

3 We must see ourselves as sojourners passing through, not as permanent residents.

4 This shattering of our assumed future happens in an instant.

5 One moment, you're making long-term plans as if you'll be here forever—committing to distant futures, collecting things you can't take with you.

6 The next moment, that illusion dissolves, replaced by a sharp awareness that you're just passing through.

7 It's the collapse of permanence—suddenly, your journey appears in its true, temporary nature.

8 The ancient Stoics practiced remembering death—reminding themselves they were mortal sojourners, not immortal residents—as a way to focus on what truly matters on the journey.

9 There's a huge difference between just knowing in your head that we're temporary visitors in this world and truly feeling this reality deep in your soul during a moment of sudden awareness.

10 One is simply a mental exercise; the other completely transforms how you see your entire life journey.

4 When we first realize this truth, something curious happens

in our minds—we can somehow be both sojourner and settler at the same time.

2 Our awareness splits in two—part of our mind continues to build as if for forever while another part now knows these are just temporary shelters.

3 After nearly dying, you might go back to your daily routines while part of your mind now sees these routines as customs of a foreign land you're just passing through.

4 When you see someone die, especially someone close to you, you might continue your normal activities while also deeply understanding how temporary everything is.

5 This split serves an important purpose—it lets you continue your necessary daily activities while absorbing the truth that you're just visiting here, not staying permanently.

6 But it also marks the beginning of a new relationship with your journey, with a heightened awareness that you're just passing through.

7 What many spiritual traditions have tried to teach through practice suddenly arrives, forcing you to recognize your true state as a sojourner.

8 In these moments, you transform how you see your journey—not as living somewhere forever but as a meaningful pilgrimage with a beginning, middle, and end.

9 These moments stand as markers on your path, showing where your understanding of life itself has fundamentally changed.

5 Waking up to your status as a sojourner creates a break not just in time but in who you are.

2 The person you were before—who built and planned as if for forever suddenly seems like a stranger, someone you used to be.

3 It raises the question: what makes you the same person at different points of your journey?

4 After such an awakening, this question becomes deeply personal: are you the same person you were before this realization?

5 This break in identity comes with a new clarity about the path.

6 When you're newly aware of your temporary stay, you naturally strip away unnecessary baggage, suddenly reorganizing what you choose to carry.

7 Things that seemed important before—status among others, possessions you can't take with you, arguments over things you never truly owned—fall away, revealed as needless burdens on your journey.

8 It makes you rethink the difference between settling down and passing through—facing mortality forces you to reconsider how you've understood your time here.

9 Even after such moments pass, their clarity may stay with you. A brush with death, a funeral that reminds you of your own mortality, a sudden physical vulnerability—each can serve as a compass redirecting your journey toward what truly matters.

10 Yet the human mind, even after profound awakening, tends to forget we're just passing through.

11 The clarity fades, the illusion of permanence returns, until another awakening moment reminds you that you're just traveling through.

6

This clarity, while showing the true nature of your journey, comes at a cost.

2 The price of such wisdom is losing the comfortable illusion that you might stay here forever.

3 It's a wisdom few would choose if given the option. This echoes ancient insight: "Nothing profound enters a sojourner's life without bringing some burden."

4 In the hours and days after facing mortality, as the initial

shock fades, we enter a new phase of our journey. We begin to travel with new eyes—seeing both the beauty of our temporary home and its impermanence.

5 We enter a state of conscious traveling, having left behind the illusion of permanent residence but not yet fully accepting our temporary status.

6 It's in this in-between space that we face the most profound questions of our journey. How shall I travel now? What is worth carrying? What marks should I leave along my path?

7 Some say we can only journey authentically when we embrace being sojourners—accepting our temporary passage through this world. These moments force exactly this realization, though rarely by choice.

7 Different sojourners realize they're sojourners in different ways. Some through dangerous paths. Others by watching fellow sojourners reach their journey's end. Still others in moments when they see how fragile the path itself is.

2 Some seek this awareness on purpose—through wilderness journeys, through practices of simplicity and letting go, or by thinking deeply about those who have died before us.

3 However this awareness comes, those who wake up to being sojourners receive a precious gift: the chance to journey with purpose, to choose their path clearly, to travel lightly, carrying only what truly matters.

4 This doesn't make the journey's challenges or the sorrow of goodbyes any less real, but it reveals the gift hidden in this awareness—the gift of traveling consciously, however difficult the path.

5 When we embrace being sojourners, we find not despair but freedom—freedom from the burden of permanence, from the worry of endless gathering, from the illusion that our journey might never end.

6 The question becomes: how shall we travel? How do we make this brief passage meaningful? How do we journey in a way that honors both the beauty of the path and how short it is?

7 These questions form the heart of what it means to travel wisely.

8 The truth that we are sojourners— temporary residents in a world we must eventually leave—need not diminish our journey but can fill it with purpose and clarity.

9 We are all passing through a world we didn't create and cannot keep.

10 Our footprints will last for a while, then fade away.

11 Our shelters will stand for a season, then fall down.

12 Our names will be spoken for a generation, then forgotten.

13 Yet in this temporary stay, this brief journey, we can find deep meaning—not despite our brief visit but because of it. The very shortness of our stay gives each moment its importance, each meeting its significance, each choice its weight.

14 So journey well, fellow sojourner.

15 Travel lightly. Love deeply. Notice the world around you. Be kind to your fellow sojourners. Leave beautiful markers along your path.

16 And always remember the two sides of your journey— that you are both passing through and fully present, both visitor and participant, both temporary and essential to the story of this world.

17 May you, O Sojourner, love living and love life.

2

the Book of 𝔐ystery

1 Listen, people, to these words of wisdom about the Most High, whose ways we cannot fully understand.

2 God has been called by many names through the ages: the Supreme Being, the Creator, the Source, the Ultimate Reality, the Ground of Being, the Infinite.

3 In Eastern traditions, God is known as Brahman, the ultimate reality, and Paramatman, the supreme soul.

4 Among the followers of the Prophet, there are ninety-nine names for Allah, each showing a different part of the divine nature.

5 Indigenous peoples speak of the Great Spirit, while Chinese sages call God the Tao, the indescribable source of all being.

6 Yet truly, these names are just small vessels trying to hold what cannot be contained.

7 Look at the heavens, made by God's hands, and the universe that shows God's craftsmanship. The universe stretches beyond ninety-three billion light years - that's 545 septillion miles - 545,000,000,000,000,000,000,000,000.

8 If you tried to count to this number, saying one number each second, it would take you three thousand years.

9 Yet this vastness, though it amazes the mind, still has boundaries and limits.

10 How much greater then is the Lord, who made all these things?

11 God's greatness cannot be measured, and divine understanding has no limits.

12 Before the mountains formed or the seas filled with water, before stars began to burn or planets moved in their orbits, God already existed.

13 Beyond time itself, the Eternal One exists, with no beginning and no end, living in what the ancients called "the eternal now" where past, present, and future are seen all at once.

14 This mystery is beyond human understanding, yet it calls to the deepest part of our spirit, because we were created with a natural longing to connect with something greater than our limited lives.

15 Here begins the great paradox of human existence: we hunger for ultimate meaning while possessing only finite understanding, we seek absolute purpose while living in relative uncertainty.

16 Yet this is not a flaw in our design but its greatest feature—that creatures capable of asking the deepest questions have been placed in a universe that preserves its deepest secrets, creating the perfect conditions for faith, wonder, and growth.

2 People like to organize and classify everything so they can understand the world around them.

2 They create frameworks and systems of knowledge that work well for earthly matters.

3 But when they try to use these methods to understand God, they're like people trying to explain colors to the blind or music to the deaf.

4 Why do people try so hard to define and limit God? Isn't it because mystery makes us uncomfortable and uncertainty troubles our soul?

5 In today's world, people want immediate answers, looking for knowledge at the touch of a button, and have forgotten the value of holy wonder.

6 Be careful not to create a god in your own image instead of standing in awe before the mystery that goes beyond all understanding.

7 When you say, "God wants this" or "God thinks that," you speak as if the Maker of All Things thinks with a mind like yours.

8 Such talk may work as a metaphor, but if taken literally, it creates an idol too small to be worthy of worship.

9 It's like an ant describing what a human is – it might see some truths, but the fullness of reality is beyond its understanding.

10 Throughout history, the biggest mistakes about God have come not from too much humility but from too much certainty, not from admitting the limits of understanding but from claiming to fully comprehend.

11 This is a wise perception and worthy of remembering - It is between the humbleness of man and the boundless mystery of God that grace, love, and truth are found.

12 It is only upon his knees and face to the dirt that a man can stand upright and walk with a clear conscience.

13 It is the arrogance of man that leads to divisions and group think and a god of pettiness.

14 How often have conflicts started, blood been

spilled, and communities been divided because some people claimed to know exactly what God is like and what God wants?

15 The person who says, "I know exactly who God is and what God wants" has probably created a deity that mirrors their own desires, fears, and biases.

16 For the Divine Reality breaks all our categories, exceeds all our definitions, goes beyond all our concepts, and overflows all our language.

17 The wise approach God as they would approach an endless ocean—with awe for its vastness, humility before its power, openness to its mystery, and awareness that they can touch only its shore.

18 Yet touching only the shore does not make the ocean meaningless or our contact with it purposeless. Even partial connection with infinite mystery can transform finite lives completely.

19 The child who builds sandcastles at the ocean's edge is not frustrated by the inability to contain the sea—the vastness itself becomes the source of wonder, play, and growth.

20 So too can we find profound meaning in our limited but real contact with unlimited mystery, purpose in our small but genuine participation in infinite reality.

3 Think about these puzzles that confuse even the wise: How can God be both far beyond creation and closely present within it?

2 How can the Holy One be single in essence yet show up in many ways?

3 How can the Eternal One be unchanging yet active in human affairs?

4 How can the Almighty be both personal as a friend and infinite as the cosmos?

5 These seeming contradictions exist not because God is

confusing, but because divine reality goes beyond the limits of human reason.

6 Some may ask, if we cannot fully know God, what's the point of our prayers and worship?

7 Here lies a great mystery: Though we cannot fully grasp God's nature, many people throughout history have experienced God's intimate presence.

8 Just as a child benefits from the sun's warmth without knowing about its fiery furnace, we can experience divine love and guidance without fully understanding its source.

9 Consider this: our inability to fully understand God isn't a failure of our minds but a testament to God's boundless nature. It's not just that our minds are too small, though they are, but that God is too great.

10 Mystics speak of "learned ignorance" and "knowing by unknowing," recognizing that the journey toward understanding God paradoxically leads to a place beyond understanding, where knowledge gives way to experience.

11 Even sacred texts acknowledge this mystery. Didn't Moses meet God in thick darkness? Wasn't Elijah met not in earthquake, wind or fire, but in quiet stillness? Didn't Paul talk about "seeing through a glass, darkly"?

12 These were not experiences of complete understanding but of life-changing presence, not of mastering divine knowledge but of being mastered by divine love.

13 The greatest saints and wise people throughout history have not been those who claimed to fully understand God but those who allowed themselves to be fully grasped by God.

14 This raises a crucial insight: meaning and purpose do not require complete understanding. The mother loves her child without comprehending the full mystery of consciousness. The artist creates beauty without understanding the ultimate nature of creativity itself.

15 Similarly, we can live with profound purpose even while

embracing profound mystery. Our calling is not to solve the riddle of existence but to participate faithfully in its unfolding.

16 The very limitations of our understanding become gateways to deeper forms of meaning—meaning found not in intellectual mastery but in trusting relationship, not in final answers but in faithful questions.

17 Consider how the most meaningful relationships in human life are with people we never fully understand. The friend who surprises us, the spouse who continues to reveal new depths, the child who grows beyond our expectations—it is precisely their mystery that keeps these relationships alive and growing.

18 If complete understanding were necessary for meaning, all relationships would die in familiarity. Instead, mystery preserves the space for continued discovery, growth, and deepening connection.

4 When you stop trying to fully understand what cannot be understood, a great peace will come to your spirit.

2 Instead of worrying about having the right doctrine, you will live in wonder and awe before the Divine Mystery.

3 Instead of arguing about whose understanding of God is right, you will see how different traditions are like blind people describing different parts of the same elephant.

4 This ancient story teaches that each perspective holds truth, yet none sees the whole picture.

5 This doesn't mean abandoning religious practices or the study of sacred matters. Instead, hold your understanding with humility, knowing your knowledge is like a lamp in the darkness – giving light to your path but not lighting up all creation.

6 Don't be afraid to say, "I don't know," and live peacefully with questions that have no answers in this mortal life.

7 The wise from many nations have taught this holy not-knowing throughout the ages.

8 The Eastern sage wrote, "The Tao that can be spoken is not the eternal Tao."

9 Jewish mystics speak of Ein Sof, the Infinite One beyond all attributes and descriptions.

10 Meister Eckhart said that the highest name for God is no name at all.

11 The Sufis teach that Allah's essence remains beyond knowledge, even as His presence guides the faithful.

12 The Desert Fathers and Mothers sought God in silence and solitude, finding that as words decreased, awareness of divine presence increased.

13 The Hindu tradition speaks of neti, neti—not this, not that—acknowledging that whatever we can think of is not the ultimate reality.

14 These diverse witnesses across traditions and centuries point to a common understanding: that God transcends all human categories while remaining intimately accessible to human experience.

15 When you release the need to understand what cannot be understood, you create space for encounter.

16 When you give up the demand for certainty, you open yourself to mystery.

17 When you let go of your concepts of God, you may begin to experience God's presence.

18 This embrace of mystery, far from making life meaningless, opens doorways to forms of meaning unavailable to those who demand complete understanding.

19 Mystery becomes the fertile soil in which purpose grows—not the sterile purpose of a predetermined plan that we must discover and follow perfectly, but the living purpose that emerges from faithful response to each moment's invitation.

20 In this way, uncertainty itself becomes a form of freedom. If everything were already determined and fully knowable, there would be no space for genuine choice, authentic growth, or creative response.

21 Mystery preserves the possibility that our choices matter, that our love has meaning, that our lives can contribute something unique to the cosmic story still being written.

22 The businessman who cannot fully understand market forces still finds meaning in serving customers well. The teacher who cannot comprehend how learning happens still finds purpose in creating conditions where it might occur.

23 Similarly, we can live with profound purpose even while swimming in an ocean of mystery, finding meaning not in what we know but in how we respond to what we encounter.

5 How then should we live with this divine mystery? Listen to this advice:

2 Embrace wonder rather than certainty. When you see a sunset, a newborn child, or the night sky filled with stars, let your heart fill with awe at the mystery of creation.

3 In such moments, you come closer to divine reality than through carefully reasoned arguments and definitions.

4 Wonder itself becomes a form of worship, a recognition that we exist within something far greater and more beautiful than our minds can fully grasp.

5 Seek to experience divine presence rather than explanation. Through prayer, meditation, contemplation, or time in nature, you may know God without fully understanding.

6 The deepest spiritual wisdom does not come through intellect alone but through direct experience of holy presence.

7 Experience provides its own form of knowledge—not the knowledge that can be written in books but the knowledge

that transforms how you live, love, and see the world.

8 Hold your beliefs with humility, seeing them as signposts pointing toward truth rather than truth itself.

9 This will help you respect your neighbors' faith and open your heart to wisdom from many sources.

10 Humility about our beliefs does not weaken their power to guide us but strengthens their ability to connect us with others who seek the same truth through different paths.

11 Find peace in accepting your limitations.

12 Just as loving parents don't expect their young children to understand the mysteries of the universe, perhaps God doesn't require that we fully comprehend divine reality.

13 Great comfort awaits those who accept that they don't need to have all the answers.

14 This acceptance liberates energy previously spent in anxious seeking for certainty, freeing it for more meaningful pursuits—loving well, serving others, creating beauty, building justice.

15 Practice the discipline of silence.

16 In our age of constant noise and endless words, create quiet spaces where you might sense the subtle presence of God beyond language.

17 For it's often in silence that the illusion of separation between human and divine begins to dissolve, and we experience ourselves as held within a greater Reality.

18 Silence creates space not just for mystery but for meaning to emerge—the kind of meaning that comes not from external explanation but from internal recognition of our place in the larger story.

19 Cultivate paradoxical thinking.

20 Learn to hold seemingly opposite truths in creative tension rather than forcing artificial resolution.

21 Divine reality often reveals itself in "both/and" rather than "either/or."

22 The One who is both beyond us and within us, both hidden and revealed, calls us to expand our minds beyond yes-or-no thinking.

23 Paradox preserves space for mystery while allowing meaningful engagement with reality. We can act decisively while acknowledging uncertainty, love completely while accepting limits, commit deeply while remaining open to new understanding.

24 Approach sacred texts and traditions as windows rather than walls. Let them open your view to divine reality rather than confining God within their boundaries. Honor their wisdom while recognizing that the map is not the territory.

25 For even the most profound religious teachings are human attempts to express encounters with a Reality that ultimately exceeds expression.

26 Sacred texts become most meaningful when understood not as final answers but as invitations to our own encounter with the mysteries they attempt to describe.

27 Find God in loving relationships. If Divine Reality is fundamentally relational—as many traditions suggest—then genuine connection with others opens paths to divine encounter that intellectual pursuit alone cannot provide.

28 As the apostle wrote, "No one has ever seen God; if we love one another, God lives in us, and his love is perfected in us."

29 In loving relationships, we often experience meanings that cannot be fully explained but are undeniably real—the purpose found in caring for another, the significance discovered in being truly known, the transformation that occurs through forgiveness given and received.

30 These experiences of meaning within mystery point toward the possibility that life's ultimate meaning may be found not in solving its riddles but in participating fully in its relationships and responsibilities.

6 The mystery of the Most High, far from being a problem for faith, becomes the foundation of deeper communion with the Divine.

2 When you release the need to understand and control everything, you open yourself to that which is greater than your definitions and concepts can contain.

3 In this embrace of holy mystery, you will find not confusion but clarity, not anxiety but peace, not bondage but freedom.

4 As the wise teacher Paul Tillich said, God is the *Ground of Being* — that which underlies all existence and meaning.

5 Perhaps your calling is not to fully understand this ground but to root yourself within it, to be sustained by it, and to grow in relationship with it.

6 In doing so, you may discover that the peace you seek comes not from having all answers, but from resting in the questions.

7 This resting in questions opens space for a different kind of meaning to emerge—meaning that comes not from knowing your destiny but from trusting your response to each moment's invitation.

8 Consider how the most meaningful human activities often involve accepting mystery while taking purposeful action within it.

9 The parent raises a child without knowing who that child will become, finding meaning in the faithful offering of love and guidance.

10 The healer treats patients without fully understanding how healing occurs, finding purpose in alleviating suffering and promoting wellness.

11 The artist creates without completely comprehending the source of inspiration, discovering meaning in the act of bringing beauty into existence.

12 In each case, mystery and meaning interweave—the mystery preserving space for authentic choice and creative response, the meaning emerging from faithful engagement with responsibilities and opportunities.

13 So too in the spiritual life: we can live with profound purpose even while acknowledging our limited understanding of ultimate reality.

14 Our purpose need not be assigned from outside but can emerge from within as we respond authentically to the needs, opportunities, and relationships we encounter.

15 Mystery ensures that this purpose remains alive and growing rather than fixed and dead. If we knew everything, there would be nothing left to discover, no space for growth, no possibility of surprise.

16 But because we live within mystery, every day offers potential for new insight, deeper love, and expanded understanding of what it might mean to live well.

17 The uncertainty that initially seems threatening becomes the very condition that makes authentic life possible—preserving space for faith rather than mere knowledge, for love rather than mere calculation, for hope rather than mere prediction.

18 In this light, mystery reveals itself not as the enemy of meaning but as its protector, not as the obstacle to purpose but as its enabler.

19 Blessed are those who find peace in what cannot be defined, for they shall know the Divine not as an object of knowledge, but as the very breath of life.

20 Blessed are those who discover meaning within mystery, for they shall find that their purpose grows larger and more beautiful as their understanding remains humble and open.

21 Blessed are those who live purposefully while accepting uncertainty, for they shall experience the deep satisfaction of faithful response to mystery's invitation.

22 Go now in peace, carrying these words in your heart, knowing that you need not solve life's riddles to live life well, need not understand everything to love deeply, need not have all answers to serve meaningfully.

23 For meaning and mystery are not enemies but dance partners, not opponents but collaborators in the grand adventure of conscious existence within an ultimately mysterious but fundamentally meaningful universe.

24 Amen.

3

the Book of Stewards

1 Think about humanity's place in this vast creation, for we are just passing through, neither masters nor makers of the universe we live in.

2 From dust we came, and to dust we will return. Our time between birth and death is just a short visit on the earth.

3 Look up at the countless stars spread across the night sky. They were here long before you were born and will continue long after you're gone. Their light travels great distances, telling stories of worlds and times beyond what you can understand.

4 The mountains rose from the depths through mighty forces, shaped by wind and water over ages. They stood watching as creatures lived and died, as species came and went, long before humans walked the earth.

5 The ancient forests grew from seeds scattered by wind and animals, building complex relationships over thousands of years. Their roots reach deep into soil made from countless generations of life that came before.

6 The oceans that cover much of our world hold mysteries we haven't yet discovered, depths we haven't explored, and life forms we haven't named. Their currents have flowed since before human memory, their tides pulled by the moon in a dance older than our oldest stories.

7 And you, human, were born into this world that you didn't make.

8 You didn't create the air you breathe, the water you drink, the soil that grows your food, or the complex web of life that keeps you alive.

9 You didn't establish the laws of nature that govern everything, from how planets move to how cells divide within your body.

10 You didn't put the stars in the sky or lay the foundations of the earth.

11 Let the sojourner understand their place: neither creator nor owner, but participant and witness, passing through a reality too vast to measure.

2 Throughout history, humans have been tempted to think they might become like gods, masters of all they study, holders of ultimate knowledge, wielders of unchallenged power.

2 This temptation takes many forms. Some build great monuments and carve their names on them, hoping to live forever through stone and memory.

3 Some gather great wealth and possessions, as if having more things might protect them from the certainty of death.

4 Some try to bend nature completely to their will, seeing rivers, forests, and animals as resources to use up rather than relationships to honor.

5 Some create terrible weapons of destruction, wielding death as if they had the right to decide who lives and who dies.

6 Some claim special knowledge of God's will, putting themselves above others, giving judgment rather than compassion, creating division rather than community.

7 Some worship their own intelligence, believing their understanding and wisdom are completely enough.

8 Yet all these pursuits end the same way.

9 The monuments crumble, the wealth passes to others, nature bears scars but continues beyond human plans, the weapons bring suffering to both those who use them and their victims, the claims of special knowledge fade as new understanding emerges, and the mind eventually faces mysteries it cannot solve.

10 For man is not a god, though they may forget this truth.

11 We did not create life, cannot stop death, did not establish the universe, cannot fully understand it, did not write the laws of nature, and cannot permanently break them.

12 The man who believes they are a god builds his house on shifting sand. When the inevitable storms come—illness, loss, failure, or simply time passing—this foundation cannot hold.

13 Therefore, let the sojourner remember: to claim godhood is to embrace illusion.

14 It leads not to rising up but to isolation, not to fulfillment but to emptiness, not to meaning but to despair.

3 Just like the illusion of godhood, there is also the illusion of ownership, the belief that the soujourner can truly own parts of a world they are merely passing through.

2 Think about what it means to claim ownership. Does the one who says "This land is mine" truly create the soil,

direct the rainfall, command the seeds to grow? Does the one who says "This knowledge is mine" truly build the human mind, create language, or make the phenomena their knowledge describes?

3 Even the things we think we own most completely—our bodies, our thoughts, our time—are not truly ours to command. Bodies age and change despite our wishes, thoughts come uninvited, and time passes whether we want it to or not.

4 The claiming of ownership has caused many sorrows throughout human history.

5 Nations have fought wars over boundaries drawn on maps, forgetting that the earth itself has no such lines.

7 People have fought over resources, forgetting that oil, minerals, and forests formed long before human hands tried to claim them.

8 People have kept knowledge to themselves instead of sharing it, thinking they'll gain more if information is rare rather than freely available.

9 They've put up barriers around ideas and created laws to stop them from spreading freely, as if thoughts could really be caged.

10 The illusion of ownership divides humans, creating artificial rankings based on who controls what.

11 It turns attention toward gathering and protecting rather than relating and contributing.

12 It creates fear of loss rather than joy in sharing.

13 A man carrying water through the desert who refuses to share with fellow human being has not secured their position but weakened it.

14 For in community there is strength, in sharing there is security, and in generosity there is abundance.

15 Therefore, let the sojourner understand: we own nothing permanently.

16 We are borrowers, not owners; caretakers, not masters; participants in a great circulation of gifts that existed before us and will continue after us.

4 If the sojourner is neither god nor owner, then what is their true role in existence?

2 Look to the ancient wisdom that speaks of humans as tenders of the garden, caretakers rather than creators, stewards rather than gods.

3 This understanding begins with humility—recognizing that the sojourner stands within a reality much greater than themselves, a participant in a world they did not design and cannot fully control.

4 Yet humility doesn't mean insignificance. The hand that tends the garden doesn't create the soil or command the seed to sprout, but through careful attention and thoughtful action, it creates conditions where life can flourish.

5 The careful gardener watches before acting, seeking to understand the needs of different plants, the patterns of weather, the relationships between soil, water, sun, and animals. The careful gardener works with these relationships rather than against them.

6 So too should the sojourner approach their brief time in the world—as one who observes carefully, listens deeply, and acts thoughtfully within a complex web of relationships they didn't create but can help nurture.

7 This role extends beyond the natural world to the realm of knowledge and understanding.

8 For knowledge, like a garden, needs tending. It must be cultivated through careful observation, nurtured through questioning and testing, shared with others who might build upon it, and protected from the weeds of falsehood and distortion.

9 The sojourner tends the garden of knowledge not by claiming ownership or authority, but by contributing their

unique perspective and receiving the perspectives of others, knowing that truth emerges most fully through many voices.

10 In both the natural world and the realm of knowledge, the sojourner who understands their role as tender of the garden approaches their task with reverence, patience, and care, recognizing that they serve something greater than themselves.

5 How then shall the sojourner live as a tender of the garden? What practices mark the path of one who sees themselves not as god or owner but as steward and caretaker?

2 Practice observation before intervention.

3 The hasty gardener who doesn't study the land before planting often wastes both seed and effort.

4 So too the sojourner must learn to observe carefully—the natural systems that sustain life, the human systems that organize society, and the patterns of their own thoughts and actions.

5 Practice humility in knowledge.

6 The garden of understanding grows beyond any single tender's oversight.

7 No one can claim to have discovered all there is to know or to have the final word on important matters. Each perspective is partial, each understanding incomplete.

8 Practice generosity in sharing.

9 The fruits of the garden are not meant for one alone but for the nourishment of many.

10 So too should the sojourner share freely what they have learned, discovered, or created, so others might benefit and build upon their work.

11 Practice gratitude for our inheritance.

12 The sojourner enters a garden already growing, tends it for a time, and passes it on to others.

13 All that we know, all that we have, all that we accomplish builds upon the efforts of countless others who came before us and shared the fruits of their labor.

14 Practice care for what continues.

15 The garden will remain after the current tender has departed.

16 The thoughtful sojourner considers not just immediate harvest but future growth, planting trees whose shade they will never sit under, preserving resources they will never use.

17 Practice community over isolation.

18 The garden grows best when many hands share in its tending, each contributing according to their gifts and abilities.

19 The sojourner who tries to tend all alone soon finds the task beyond their strength.

20 Practice restoration where there is damage.

21 Where the garden has been harmed through neglect or exploitation, the tender works to heal and regenerate, knowing that living things have remarkable ability to renew themselves when given proper conditions and care.

6 The path of the sojourner who seeks to be a tender of the garden is not without difficulty. Many forces work against this understanding, pulling the sojourner toward illusions of godhood and ownership.

2 There is the challenge of ego, which whispers that you are special, separate, superior to other sojourners, tempting you to place your name and needs above the wellbeing of the garden itself.

3 There is the challenge of fear, which warns that there is not enough, that you must secure your portion against others, that generosity leads to scarcity rather than abundance.

4 There is the challenge of impatience, which urges immediate results rather than careful cultivation, taking rather than regenerating, shortcuts instead of sustainable practices.

5 There is the challenge of distraction, which pulls attention away from the garden toward artificial pursuits, trivial concerns, and endless consumption, leaving little time or energy for the work of tending.

6 There is the challenge of despair, which suggests that the garden is beyond repair, that the damage done is too great, that the efforts of one sojourner or even many cannot make a meaningful difference.

7 There is the challenge of isolation, which separates tender from tender, breaking the community that gives strength and resilience to the work of stewardship.

8 Yet the sojourner who recognizes these challenges can meet them.

9 The ego can be balanced with humility, fear with trust, impatience with perseverance, distraction with presence, despair with hope, and isolation with community.

7 As the sojourner tends the garden, the garden also tends the sojourner. For in this relationship of care and stewardship, wisdom grows alongside the plants and knowledge.

2 The garden teaches patience, for no amount of worry or haste can make a seed sprout before its time.

3 The rhythms of growth and death, bloom and wilting, follow their own necessary timing.

4 The garden teaches interdependence, for no plant grows entirely alone. Each depends on soil organisms, pollinators, and other plants in a complex web of relationships. So too does the sojourner exist within webs of relationships and mutual support.

5 The garden teaches resilience, for after fire and flood, drought and disease, life returns in new forms, finding paths to expression even in challenging conditions. This resilience offers hope to the sojourner facing difficulties.

6 The garden teaches the wisdom of limits, for every plant has particular needs for sun, water, and nutrients. To thrive, they must have neither too much nor too little of each. So too does the sojourner need to find balance rather than excess.

7 The garden teaches the beauty of diversity, for a single-

crop planting is vulnerable to disease and pests in ways that diverse plantings are not. Different species support each other's growth, just as different perspectives and traditions enrich human understanding.

8 The garden teaches the reality of change, for no garden remains static. Seasons turn, plants grow and die, soil transforms, and new relationships emerge.

9 The tender who resists all change soon finds themselves fighting the very nature of life itself.

10 Above all, the garden teaches the sojourner that they are part of something greater than themselves—a living, changing, complex reality that existed before them and will continue after them, in which they play an important but temporary role.

8

Though the sojourner's time in the garden of life is brief, their tending leaves traces that continue beyond their journey.

2 Consider, then, what legacy you wish to leave in the garden entrusted temporarily to your care.

3 Will you leave the soil more alive or depleted? Will you leave the waters cleaner or more polluted? Will you leave the air purer or more contaminated? Will you leave greater or less diversity of life? These questions apply to both the literal earth and to the communities and cultures we inhabit.

4 In the garden of knowledge, will you leave greater understanding or more confusion? Will you leave bridges between different ways of knowing or walls that separate them? Will you leave questions that invite further exploration or dogmas that close off questions?

5 In the garden of human relationships, will you leave more compassion or more indifference? More trust or more suspicion? More healing or more damage?

6 Remember that the sojourner doesn't need to transform the entire garden in one lifetime. Even small acts of careful

tending matter. A single tree planted, a single stream protected, a single species preserved, a single truth spoken, a single injustice confronted, a single relationship healed—these are no small things in the continuity of care that sustains the garden.

7 Remember also that you tend the garden alongside many others, both those who came before and those who will come after, as well as your fellow sojourners in the present. Your work connects to theirs in ways you may never fully know.

8 Therefore, tend with intention but without attachment to outcomes.

9 Plant seeds without demanding to see all they will become.

10 Trust that careful stewardship creates possibilities beyond what any single tender can envision.

11 For the greatest legacy of the tender is not what they personally accomplish or accumulate, but how well they participate in the ongoing growth of a reality greater than themselves—a reality they did not create and do not own, but in which they play a meaningful part during their brief journey.

12 Let the sojourner understand: We are neither gods nor owners, but tenders of a garden.

13 As tenders of the garden, we find our true purpose, dignity, and belonging as we pass through this world, caring for what has been entrusted to us and preparing to pass it on to those who will follow.

4
the Book of Expectations

1 Think about the path we walk through this world, and the expectations that grow in our hearts about goodness, kindness, and right actions.

2 Many people go through life believing their good deeds should be rewarded, their kindness should be repaid, and their sacrifices should be honored and remembered.

3 They give expecting something in return, help expecting gratitude, and sacrifice hoping for recognition. When these expectations aren't met, bitterness grows in their hearts.

4 But look at the trees in the field, which give shade to everyone who passes under them without asking who deserves it. Look at the rain, which falls on the fields of both thankful and unthankful farmers.

5 Does the sun demand thanks for its warmth? Does the stream expect praise for its cool water? Does the soil require acknowledgment for supporting the seed? These give according to their nature, without expecting reward.

6 In the same way, goodness is the natural state of the person who understands their place in the greater pattern of existence. It's not a special gift deserving reward but the normal expression of one who sees clearly.

7 For what is goodness but living in harmony with the true nature of things? What is kindness but recognizing our connection with all that lives? What is right action but moving in harmony with the deeper current of reality?

8 The person who demands reward for basic goodness is like someone who expects payment for breathing, or recognition for having a heartbeat. These aren't special achievements but the natural functioning of a human life.

2 Throughout their journey, people encounter the persistent illusion of deserving—the belief that the universe operates on principles of fairness and just payment for goodness.

2 This illusion takes many forms. Some believe wealth should flow to the righteous and hardship to the wicked.

3 Some expect suffering should match wrongdoing and joy should match righteousness.

4 Some imagine an invisible ledger where good deeds add up like money, to be exchanged for blessings and protection against misfortune.

5 Some become angry when tragedy strikes them despite their good living.

6 But look at the world as it is, not as human minds wish it to be.

7 The storm doesn't avoid the house of the generous person. Disease doesn't spare the forgiving. Age doesn't slow its effects on the bodies of the kind.

8 The workings of the physical world—the movement of earth's plates, the division of cells, the changing of viruses, the patterns of weather—operate according to their own principles, not according to human ideas of worth and reward.

9 The social world too, with all its complexities and imperfections, doesn't guarantee that kindness will be met with kindness, that honesty will be rewarded with success, that sacrifice will be honored with recognition.

10 The person who bases their goodness on expectations of reward builds their house on shifting sand.

11 When the inevitable storms come—ingratitude, misunderstanding, or simple indifference—this foundation cannot hold.

12 Therefore, let people release the illusion of deserving.

13 Good flows from goodness itself, not from expecting reward.

14 Right action is its own justification, needing no external validation or cosmic balancing.

3 If goodness deserves no special reward, why then should we persist in kindness, compassion, and right action? Because these aren't optional virtues but necessary expressions of our true nature and condition.

2 Consider: You didn't create yourself. Your existence depends on countless others—those who cared for you in childhood, those who grow your food, those who built the buildings you live in, those who came before and developed the knowledge you rely on.

3 Your very breath depends on forests and oceans you didn't create. Your health depends on immune systems you didn't design. Your consciousness emerged from processes you didn't start.

4 In light of this basic interconnection, goodness isn't a special achievement but the appropriate response to reality.

5 Gratitude isn't an exceptional virtue but an accurate perception.

6 Generosity isn't sacrifice but participation in the circulation of gifts that sustains all life.

7 The person who withholds goodness is like a cell that refuses to contribute to the body that houses it, like a branch that tries to hoard sunlight from the tree that supports it, like a river that tries to prevent its waters from joining the sea.

8 Such withholding doesn't lead to advantage but to isolation, not to gain but to loss, not to security but to weakness.

9 For we are made for connection and contribution, not for separation and hoarding.

10 Therefore, understand: We practice goodness not to earn rewards but because it aligns us with reality.

11 We act with compassion not to build up points but because compassion fits our condition.

12 We live with generosity not to secure future benefits but because generous participation in life is why we are here.

4 As we travel through this world, suffering appears in many forms—physical pain, emotional distress, loss, disappointment, illness, and ultimately, death.

2 No life is untouched by suffering, regardless of virtue or vice.

3 Some suffering comes from the nature of physical existence itself. Bodies age and decay according to biological processes. Cells copy themselves imperfectly over time. Systems gradually lose their resilience and functionality.

4 Some suffering comes from the structure of a world in constant change. What forms must eventually dissolve. What rises must eventually fall. What comes together must eventually separate.

5 Attachment to permanence in an impermanent reality creates inevitable pain.

6 Some suffering comes from the complexity of human interconnection. Misunderstandings arise. Needs conflict. Perspectives differ. Even with the best intentions, humans hurt one another through ignorance, fear, or simple limitation.

7 Some suffering comes from our own mind—from wanting what cannot be, from rejecting what must be, from expecting what reality doesn't provide, from holding onto what must be released.

8 The person who expects a life without suffering misunderstands the fundamental nature of the journey.

9 It's not that suffering is good or necessary in some cosmic plan, but that it's inevitable given the conditions of physical existence in a changing world.

10 Yet this recognition need not lead to despair. For suffering, while inevitable, isn't the whole story of our journey. It's one thread in a complex tapestry that also includes beauty, connection, wonder, and joy.

5 How then shall we relate to the suffering that appears on our path?

2 Not with denial or avoidance, for these only delay and often intensify the experience.

3 Not with excessive fear or anticipation, for these add unnecessary suffering to the inevitable.

4 Rather, meet suffering with clear seeing. Much unnecessary pain comes from resisting what is already present, from telling stories about why this shouldn't be happening, from comparing your journey with imagined alternatives.

5 The person who can simply acknowledge "This is suffering" without adding "This shouldn't be" or "This is unfair" has already reduced their burden.

6 Clear seeing doesn't eliminate pain but removes the additional weight of arguing with reality.

7 Meet suffering with appropriate response. Some pain can be addressed through action—seeking medical care for illness, making amends for harm caused, adjusting course when a path leads to damage.

8 The wise sojourner distinguishes between what can be changed and what must be accepted.

9 Meet suffering with compassion.

10 When pain can't be avoided or immediately resolved, it can still be accompanied with kindness rather than judgment, with gentle attention rather than anxiety or numb detachment.

11 Meet suffering with perspective.

12 Even intense pain is rarely constant or permanent. It rises, changes, and eventually passes, like weather moving through the sky.

13 The sojourner who sees the changing nature of experience knows that no condition, pleasant or unpleasant, represents the entirety of life.

14 Meet suffering with connection rather than isolation.

15 Shared pain becomes more bearable. The support of fellow sojourners provides both practical assistance and the profound comfort of knowing you're not alone in your difficulty.

16 In these ways, we learn that while suffering can't be eliminated from the journey, it can be met with wisdom that transforms how it's experienced and what it creates in our life.

6 Between birth and death, between joy and sorrow, between gain and loss, we encounter countless moments of potential beauty, peace, and happiness. These moments arise not despite the challenges of the journey but interwoven with them.

2 There is the beauty of dawn breaking over mountains, of light playing on water, of a child's laughter, of music that stirs deep feelings, of human faces lined with years of experience.

3 This beauty asks only to be noticed, not fixed or preserved or improved.

4 There is the peace of quiet connection with another being, of solitude in natural settings, of work that engages your full capacity, of rest after meaningful effort, of acceptance after struggle.

5 This peace emerges not from perfect circumstances but from alignment with what is.

6 There is the happiness of simple pleasures—the taste of fruit, the warmth of sun on skin, the comfort of shelter during the storm, the satisfaction of thirst quenched by cool water.

7 This happiness requires no extraordinary achievement or acquisition, only presence with ordinary experience.

8 And beyond these earthly pleasures, there are sacred moments when we sense the presence of the Creator who set this journey in motion.

9 In stillness, in wonder, in gratitude, in awe—the veil between worlds grows thin, and we experience connection with the divine source of all existence.

10 These moments of divine presence may come unexpectedly—in the majesty of nature, in the depths of prayer or meditation when thoughts grow quiet, in the experience of love that seems to come from beyond human ability, in encounters with beauty so profound it brings awe.

11 In such moments, we taste a peace that surpasses understanding, a joy not dependent on circumstance, a love not limited by human weakness.

12 These are not moments of escape from reality but of deeper immersion in it—glimpses of the depth of being that underlies all creation.

13 These moments are not rewards for goodness or compensation for suffering. They are simply part of the landscape of any human journey, available to all who have developed the ability to recognize and receive them.

14 The ability to recognize and receive is not automatic. It must be cultivated through intention and practice.

15 The person whose attention is constantly fixed on the destination may miss the beauty of the path.

16 The individual obsessed with acquiring may overlook the richness of what is freely given.

17 The pilgrim distracted by noise and activity may miss the still, small voice that speaks in the silence.

18 Therefore, let us develop the arts of noticing, appreciating, and savoring the moments of beauty, peace, and happiness that arise naturally in any life, and especially those sacred moments of divine presence that nourish the spirit and remind us of our true home.

7

How shall we cultivate the ability to recognize and fully experience the moments of beauty, peace, and happiness that appear along our path, especially those sacred moments in the presence of the Creator?

2 Practice being present with what is, rather than constantly comparing with what might be.

3 The mind that is always elsewhere—rehashing the past, planning the future, imagining alternatives—misses the richness of the only moment that truly exists: this one.

4 In this present moment alone do we encounter the eternal presence of the Creator.

5 Practice gratitude not as obligation but as clear perception.

6 The sojourner who notices what is going well, what is supporting their journey, what is offering beauty or connection or comfort, experiences a life much richer than one who notices only lacks and problems.

7 Gratitude opens the heart to receive the divine presence that always surrounds us but often goes unnoticed.

8 Practice slowing down enough to actually experience your experiences.

9 A life lived at constant speed and urgent pace becomes a blur, with moments of potential depth reduced to items checked off a list, barely acknowledged before moving to the next task or concern.

10 The voice of the Creator is rarely heard in the whirlwind but often in the gentle whisper that requires stillness to perceive.

11 Practice directing attention intentionally rather than letting it be constantly captured by whatever is loudest—whether external demands and distractions or internal worries and thoughts.

12 Attention is the doorway to experience; where attention goes, life follows.

13 The person who regularly turns attention toward the divine discovers that this awareness gradually fills all of life.

14 Practice savoring—the art of staying with pleasant experience long enough to fully receive it, to let it register in awareness and body, to appreciate its qualities and effects, before moving on to the next moment.

15 Savoring becomes especially powerful in moments of divine connection, allowing the transformative presence to fill life more deeply.

16 Practice sacred pause—intentionally setting aside time for private communion with the Creator through prayer, meditation, contemplation, or simply attentive silence.

17 Sacred pauses create an opening for divine encounter and develop the sensitivity to recognize sacred moments throughout ordinary life.

18 Practice seeing with eyes of faith—recognizing that what appears merely physical or mundane to ordinary perception may be filled with divine presence when seen through spiritual awareness.

19 The burning bush is always present; what's needed are eyes prepared to see it.

20 Practice sharing beauty, peace, and happiness when they appear.

21 Experiences deepen when communicated.

22 The person who says to a companion "Look at that sunset" or "Listen to this music" or "Taste how delicious this is" doubles their own joy while creating connection.

23 So it is with spiritual experience—when shared in community, divine encounters strengthen both the individual and the community.

24 Practice finding beauty, peace, and happiness even in challenging circumstances.

25 The ability to notice a bird singing outside a hospital window, to appreciate the kindness of a stranger during a difficult time, to feel moments of calm amid chaos—these represent not denial of reality but a more complete perception of it.

26 So too, the practice of finding God's presence even in darkness and difficulty transforms suffering from mere endurance to potential communion.

27 When we regularly practice these arts of presence, we discover that moments in the Creator's presence bring unique results—a centeredness that persists amid chaos, a compassion that flows more naturally, a clarity about what truly matters, a courage to face difficulty, a lessening of fear, and a sense of being held in something greater than oneself.

28 Moments of divine connection gradually reshape us from within.

29 One who has tasted the presence of God becomes less attached to passing pleasures, less disturbed by temporary setbacks, more rooted in what endures, more capable of seeing the sacred within the ordinary. This is not withdrawal from life but deeper immersion in its true nature.

8 As we integrate these understandings—that goodness deserves no special reward, that suffering is natural to the journey, that moments of beauty and joy are available to be seized—a deeper wisdom emerges: the wisdom of non-entitlement.

2 The person who has released the illusion of deserving discovers an unexpected freedom.

3 No longer believing that life owes them happiness for their goodness, they can receive happiness when it appears as a pure gift rather than a partial payment of a debt.

4 No longer expecting that goodness should shield them from suffering, they can meet difficulties with resilience rather than bewildered outrage.

5 No longer keeping score of their contributions and the world's responses, they can give freely without the poison of resentment.

6 This wisdom of non-entitlement doesn't lead to passiveness or resignation but to engagement with life as it actually is, rather than as human minds believe it should be.

7 It leads not to reduced motivation for good but to purified motivation, goodness for its own sake rather than for anticipated rewards.

8 The person who embodies this wisdom becomes like a tree by the water, drawing nourishment from the depths regardless of whether its fruit is picked with gratitude, whether its beauty is noticed, whether its shade is appreciated.

9 The tree simply lives according to its nature, doing what it does because that is what trees do.

10 This way of being brings a profound peace that doesn't depend on external conditions or fairness.

11 It is the peace of alignment with reality, of

participation in life's unfolding without the constant argument with what is.

12 Let us understand: We are not owed happiness for our goodness. We are not exempt from suffering because of our virtue.

13 We are simply sojourners through this world for a brief time, with the capacity to choose how we travel—with resistance or acceptance, with closed fists or open hands, with eyes downcast or attentive to wonder.

14 The journey involves both difficulty and delight, both struggle and grace, both giving and receiving.

15 When we embrace all of these as part of the natural experience, without entitlement or expectation, we discover a steady joy that transcends circumstances—the joy of clear seeing, open participation, and grateful presence on this extraordinary, ordinary path we all walk together.

5

the Book of Paths

1 Consider how each person journeys through this world, how no two paths are exactly the same even though many travel across the same land.

2 As each star in the night sky shines with its own light, so too does each sojourner carry a unique light on their journey.

3 The Creator has made each person with different gifts, perspectives, personalities, and purposes. There are qualities of the divine that show through your particular journey that cannot appear in quite the same way through anyone else.

4 Each of us is a unique collection of DNA, experiences, memories, personality traits, relationships, environmental factors, cultural influences, and a myriad of other elements.

5 Your specific mix of strengths and weaknesses, joys and sorrows, insights and blind spots—these aren't random but form the unique vessel through which divine light shines in this world.

6 The cracks in your vessel allow light to enter in ways that perfect vessels cannot know.

7 As rivers each find their own way to the sea, following the particular landscape they encounter, so too must each person find their authentic path according to the inner and outer terrain of their life.

8 This truth stands firm: You were not created to walk someone else's path.

9 The journey that is right for your fellow sojourner may not be right for you. The pace that helps their growth may not help yours. The lessons they need may differ from those you need.

10 Therefore, honor the sacred uniqueness of your journey.

11 Don't lessen its value through constant comparison with others who travel differently.

12 Don't abandon your authentic path to follow routes better suited to different sojourners.

13 For the person who tries to walk a path not their own experiences a deep disharmony—the friction between the life they are living and the life they were designed to live.

14 This disharmony shows up as tiredness beyond normal fatigue, as emptiness despite activity, as a subtle, persistent sense of betraying something essential.

15 Yet the uniqueness of your path doesn't mean isolation on your journey. For while each person walks their own way, no one walks entirely alone.

16 The paths of sojourners continually cross each other, running parallel for a time, then separate and come together again in the great movements of human experience.

2 Look around you on the path and see your fellow sojourners. Some walk ahead, having started earlier or moved more quickly. Some walk behind, having begun more recently or traveled more slowly. Many walk alongside, sharing this particular stretch of the journey.

2 These fellow sojourners are not obstacles to your journey but essential companions.

3 For there are stretches of the path too difficult to navigate alone, burdens too heavy for one to carry, dangers better faced together, and joys that grow when shared.

4 In the community of sojourners, wisdom accumulates.

5 Those who have walked certain terrain before can offer guidance about what lies ahead.

6 Those with different perspectives notice what you might miss.

7 Those with complementary strengths can support where you are weak.

8 In the company of fellow sojourners, accountability emerges.

9 When you stray from your authentic path, true companions will gently question your direction.

10 When you move too quickly past important landmarks, they will invite you to pause.

11 When you lose heart, they will remind you of your purpose.

12 In the fellowship of the journey, burdens are shared.

13 No sojourner can carry everything alone.

14 At times you will need to lean on the strength of others; at times they will need to lean on yours. This mutual support doesn't diminish but honors the dignity of each sojourner.

15 Therefore, receive with gratitude the gift of traveling companions.

16 Don't isolate yourself from the community of sojourners out of pride, fear, or false self-sufficiency.

17 Join your particular path to the greater flow of humanity's journey toward meaning, purpose, and connection with the divine.

18 Yet in embracing community, be watchful against losing yourself. For while isolation impoverishes the journey, so too does the loss of your unique identity in the community.

19 There is a middle path that honors both individual calling and belonging.

3 The sojourner faces many forces that would pull them from their authentic path. Some are external—the expectations of others, the pressure to conform, the attraction of approval, the weight of convention. Some are internal—fear of standing out, worry about making mistakes, doubt about one's own decision-making, the comfort of following rather than leading.

2 Consider how easily the uniqueness of your journey can be hidden. A parent insists you follow their path. A community expects you to travel as they do. A culture elevates certain journeys while dismissing others. A friend cannot understand why you must take a different route.

3 Consider also how the voice of the crowd can drown out the quieter voice within that knows your true direction. The crowd speaks with such certainty, such volume, such apparent authority. The inner voice speaks more softly, requiring stillness and attention to be heard.

4 The sojourner who surrenders their unique path to follow the crowd gains temporary comfort but loses purpose. They may be surrounded by many but paradoxically become more alone.

5 True connection happens when authentic beings meet, not when false people interact.

6 The sojourner who abandons their divine calling for social approval receives the fleeting satisfaction of others' approval but forfeits the deeper affirmation that comes from alignment with their created purpose.

7 External approval cannot fill the space meant for internal genuineness.

8 Therefore, be watchful against the subtle ways you might surrender your authentic journey. Notice when you silence your inner voice to blend with the group. Pay attention to the discomfort that arises when you betray your true path. Listen for the gentle but persistent call back to your unique way.

9 This watchfulness is not selfishness but stewardship—the careful tending of the unique vessel you were created to be and the particular light you were designed to carry.

10 Following your authentic path honors both the Creator who fashioned your distinct journey and the community that needs your authentic contribution.

4 How then shall the sojourner maintain their unique journey while remaining in life-giving connection with fellow sojourners?

2 Practice discernment between the true voice of community and the false voice of conformity.

3 The true voice of community supports your authentic unfolding while offering guidance and perspective.

4 The false voice of conformity demands sameness at the cost of authenticity.

5 Practice regular solitude and silence.

6 The sojourner who never steps apart from the crowd cannot hear their inner guidance clearly.

7 Find regular times to be alone with the Creator, to listen to your own heart, to reconnect with your particular calling before rejoining the company of others.

8 Practice expressing your own truth, even when it differs from those around you.

9 The muscle of authentic expression grows stronger with use. Begin with small truths in safe spaces, gradually developing the ability to stand in your unique perspective even in challenging situations.

10 Practice choosing companions wisely.

11 Not all fellow sojourners will honor your unique journey. Some may demand conformity as the price of connection. Some may feel threatened by your different path.

12 Seek out those who celebrate your authenticity even when it leads you in different directions.

13 Practice appropriate boundaries. The sojourner must learn when to say yes and when to say no, when to join and when to withdraw, when to adapt to others and when to hold firm. These boundaries are not walls but permeable membranes, allowing connection without loss of self.

14 Practice returning to your authentic path when you've strayed. All sojourners occasionally lose their way, following others' journeys out of fear, habit, or confusion. When you recognize this happening, gently return to your true path without harsh self-judgment for the detour.

15 Practice honoring the unique journeys of others.

16 The sojourner who respects the sacred calling of fellow sojourners creates the conditions for respect of their own path.

17 Support others in their authentic unfolding, even when their way differs from yours.

5 As you walk your authentic path while remaining in community, look for the signs of divine confirmation that you are indeed following your true journey.

2 There is a sense of resonance, of "rightness" that goes beyond logic or convenience.

3 Even when your path involves difficulty, there is an underlying peace that comes from alignment with your created purpose.

4 There is increased energy rather than depletion. The sojourner on their authentic path may tire physically but experiences a renewal of spirit that comes from living congruently. Moving against your true nature depletes; moving with it energizes.

5 There is fruit that emerges naturally. The sojourner on their authentic path finds that good things grow from their journey without forced effort—deeper connections, meaningful contributions, personal growth, quiet joy—as trees bear fruit not through straining but through being what they were created to be.

6 There is growth in love rather than self-absorption.

7 The truly authentic path always leads toward greater love —of the Creator, of others, of oneself, of the world.

8 If your journey leads toward isolation, judgment, or self-centeredness, it is not your divine path regardless of how unique it may appear.

9 There is confirmation through both inner peace and outer signs. The sojourner receives validation both through internal resonance and through external markers—doors that open, resources that appear, companions who arrive, and impact that exceeds what could be accomplished through human effort alone.

10 This confirmation comes not as reward for independence or self-reliance, but as affirmation of faithful stewardship of your particular journey, your unique vessel, your distinct light in the vast constellation of human lives.

6 At its heart, walking your own journey while in community is a spiritual practice—the art of being fully yourself as an act of devotion to the Creator who fashioned you and your path.

2 Consider: When you live your authentic journey, you express an aspect of divine creativity that no other sojourner can manifest in quite the same way.

3 Your uniqueness is not an accident but intentional.

4 Your particular blend of qualities offers the world a glimpse of the infinite divine expressed through finite human form.

5 Consider also: When you honor your true path while remaining connected to community, you participate in the great paradox of unity in diversity that reflects the nature of the Creator—the One who is also Many, the source of all creation.

6 The spiritual practice of being yourself requires both courage and humility. Courage to stand in your truth when easier paths call. Humility to recognize that your path, while uniquely yours, is one of countless equally valuable journeys and depends on wisdom beyond your own.

7 Being yourself requires both faithful listening and bold action. Listening to the quiet voice of divine guidance within. Acting with conviction even when the path ahead is unclear and others question your direction.

8 Being yourself requires both differentiation and connection. Differentiation—knowing where you end and others begin, what is your responsibility and what is not. Connection—maintaining bonds of love and community even while walking your distinct path.

9 As you practice being fully yourself on your journey, something remarkable occurs: rather than separating you from others, authentic self-expression creates the possibility of genuine community.

10 True connection happens not between masks and performances but between beings who stand in their authenticity.

7 Let the sojourner understand. Your journey has its own value, not because of status achieved or approval garnered, but because it is the path uniquely entrusted to you by the Creator.

2 The value of your journey lies partly in what it creates in you.

3 Through your particular path—with its specific challenges, joys, questions, and discoveries—you are being formed.

4 Your capacity for love, wisdom, courage, and communion with the divine deepens in ways possible only through your unique travel.

5 The value of your journey lies partly in what it offers others.

6 Your authentic path—with its distinctive insights, gifts, and perspectives—contributes something essential to the community of sojourners that would be missed if you walked another's way.

7 The value of your journey lies partly in what it reveals of the Creator.

8 Your faithful walking—staying true to your path while honoring others on theirs—makes visible an aspect of divine love and creativity that would remain hidden if you lived according to others' expectations.

9 Therefore, believe in the worth of your journey even when it seems insignificant compared to others' paths, even when progress feels slow, even when the way forward is unclear, even when few recognize the value of your particular travels.

10 The belief in the worth of your journey is not pride but faith—trust that the One who set you on this path sees its full significance even when you cannot, knows its complete purpose even when you glimpse only pieces, and values its unique contribution even when others fail to recognize it.

Here I Am

11 Walk, then, with both humble confidence and connected independence.

12 Join your particular journey to the great company of sojourners moving through this world while remaining true to your authentic path.

13 Honor the sacred worth of your unique travels while celebrating the equally valuable journeys of others.

14 For in this balance—being fully yourself while fully connected—you discover the deepest meaning of the sojourner's way: to shine your distinct light as part of the greater galaxy, to sing your unique note within the greater harmony, to walk your individual path as part of the greater journey toward the divine heart that is both our origin and our destination.

6
the Book of Wonder

1 Consider the child who sees snow for the first time—how their eyes widen, how they reach out with tentative fingers to touch this mystery falling from the sky, how they stand transfixed by the simple miracle of frozen water bouncing on the wind.

2 In that moment, they are not thinking about temperature or precipitation patterns or the inconvenience of weather. They are encountering pure wonder, the capacity to be astonished by what is.

3 This same capacity lives within every sojourner on the journey, though it often becomes buried beneath layers of explanation, expectation, and the false sophistication that mistakes knowing about something for truly seeing it.

4 Wonder is not childish naivety but reccognizing that reality is far more mysterious and magnificent than our explanations can capture.

5 It is the awareness that every ordinary moment contains extraordinary depths, that the familiar world is actually strange and marvelous when seen with fresh eyes.

6 The sojourner who cultivates wonder discovers that the journey itself becomes transformed—not just the destinations but the very act of traveling, not just the answers but the questions, not just the known but the vast territories of the unknowable.

7 For wonder is both a way of seeing and a way of being, both a practice and a gift, both the beginning of wisdom and its finest result.

2 Understand this truth: wonder is not something you either have or lack, but something you choose to cultivate or allow to wither.

2 Like a garden that will grow either flowers or weeds depending on what is planted and tended, the mind will develop either wonder or cynicism based on how attention is directed and what thoughts are nurtured.

3 Wonder requires conscious cultivation because the world seems designed to erode it—through repetition that makes the miraculous seem ordinary, through education that emphasizes analysis over appreciation, through culture that values knowing over wondering.

4 The person who sees the same sunrise every morning may stop noticing the daily miracle of light rising from darkness, color filling the sky, warmth reaching across vast space to touch their skin.

5 The student who learns how photosynthesis works may forget to marvel that plants inhale sunlight and breathe out the oxygen that keeps us alive.

6 The adult who understands the mechanics of love may miss the wonder that two separate beings can share one life, that hearts can recognize each other across crowded rooms, that caring for another can feel as natural as caring for oneself.

7 This is why wonder must be practiced deliberately, protected intentionally, and renewed regularly—not because it is weak, but because the forces that diminish it are strong and constant.

3 The practice of wonder begins with the discipline of attention—learning to truly see what is before you rather than simply recognizing what you expect to find.

2 Most of the time, we do not actually see the tree outside our window but rather notice that "tree" is still there, filing it under familiar categories without taking in its particular shape, its current condition, its unique presence in this moment.

3 We do not really see our friend's face but confirm that this is indeed our friend, missing the subtle changes that tell stories of their recent experiences, dreams, and concerns.

4 We do not truly see our food but consume it while thinking of other things, missing the colors, textures, flavors, and the remarkable journey it took to reach our plate.

5 The practice of wonder requires slowing down enough to actually perceive what we are encountering rather than simply processing it as information.

6 It means looking at familiar things as if for the first time, listening to ordinary sounds as if they were music, touching common objects as if they were treasures.

7 This is not faked or forced excitement but genuine attention to what is actually present when we stop assuming we already know everything worth knowing about our surroundings.

8 The wonderful secret is that when we truly pay attention, everything reveals layers of complexity, beauty, and mystery that casual observers never see.

4 Wonder grows in the space between knowing and not-knowing, in the recognition that every answer creates new questions, that every explanation uncovers new mysteries.

2 The person who thinks they have figured out how relationships work discovers that each new relationship teaches them how little they actually knew about love.

3 The student who masters the basics of any subject realizes how much is beyond their knowledge.

4 The parent who feels confident about raising children finds that each child requires them to learn parenting all over again.

5 This is the paradox of learning: the more you know, the more you realize you don't know. True education expands awareness of mystery rather than eliminating it.

6 Wonder is what lives in this expanded awareness—not confusion or frustration at the limits of knowledge, but appreciation for the vast richness of reality.

7 The wise person learns to love the questions as much as the answers, to find beauty in uncertainty as well as clarity, to rest comfortably in the not-knowing.

8 For wonder recognizes that mystery is not a problem to be solved but a reality to be appreciated, not a sign of ignorance but evidence of depth.

9 The person who has lost their capacity for wonder often seeks to eliminate all mystery from their life, demanding explanations for everything, becoming frustrated when life refuses to fit into neat categories.

10 But the person who lives in wonder embraces mystery as a friend, finding joy in questions that have no final answers, beauty in experiences that are beyond explanation.

5 Cynicism is wonder's primary enemy—not the honest awareness of problems or the realistic view of challenges, but the assumption that nothing is as good as it appears.

2 The cynic looks at acts of kindness and assumes hidden motives, encounters beauty and suspects manipulation, witnesses joy and expects it to be false or temporary.

3 This attitude protects against disappointment by preventing hope, shields against being fooled by refusing to believe, guards against being hurt by keeping others at emotional distance.

4 But the cost of this protection is enormous: the cynic trades the possibility of being occasionally wrong for the certainty of missing most of life's actual goodness.

5 They become like someone who wears sunglasses all the time to avoid being hurt by the bright sunlight, thus missing not only the painful glare but all the colors and beauty that only become visible in full spectrum of light.

6 Cynicism often develops as a response to being hurt by trusting too much or hoping too naively, but it overcorrects by trusting too little and hoping not at all.

7 The antidote to cynicism is not naive optimism but mature wonder—the ability to remain open to beauty and goodness while acknowledging that pain and ugliness also exist.

8 Wonder can coexist with wisdom. It does not require ignorance of problems but refuses to let problems become the whole story.

9 The person of wonder says, "Yes, there is cruelty in the world, and there is also kindness. Yes, there is ugliness, and there is also beauty. Yes, there is reason for sadness, and there is also cause for joy."

10 They choose to give equal attention to all aspects of reality rather than focusing only on what confirms their fears or disappointments.

6 One of wonder's greatest gifts is its ability to transform ordinary moments into experiences of profound meaning and connection.

2 The person who grows wonder discovers that they do not need to travel to distant places or have extraordinary experiences to encounter the miraculous—it is hidden in plain sight within everyday life.

3 They find wonder in birds in flight, in the way morning light transforms familiar rooms, in the complexity of flavors in a simple piece of fruit.

4 They are amazed at the intricate engineering of their own body—how cuts heal, how thoughts form, how emotions come and go like weather systems through the consciousness.

5 They find mystery in ordinary conversations, recognizing the miracle that sounds made by one person's mouth can create ideas in another person's mind, that invisible thoughts can be shared through visible words.

6 This transformation of the ordinary into the extraordinary does not depend on changing external circumstances but on changing internal attention.

7 The same sunrise that one person dismisses as just another day becomes for another person a daily masterpiece, a recurring gift, a moment of connection with the forces that sustain all life.

8 Wonder reveals that the difference between a magical life and a mundane one lies not in what happens but in how what happens is received, processed, and appreciated.

7 The relationship between wonder and wisdom is intimate and reciprocal.

2 Wonder leads to wisdom, and wisdom deepens wonder.

3 Wonder motivates the questions that begin the search for understanding. The child who wonders why the sky is blue

begins learning about light and the atmosphere. The person who wonders how plants grow begins discovering the mysteries of photosynthesis and the chemistry of soil.

4 But as understanding grows, so does appreciation for the beauty and complexity of what is being understood. The more you learn about how birds fly, the more amazing flight becomes. The more you understand about human consciousness, the more mysterious awareness itself appears.

5 True wisdom always increases rather than decreases wonder because it reveals how much more there is to learn, how much deeper the mysteries go, how much more magnificent reality is than our initial impressions suggested.

6 The person who has achieved superficial knowledge may lose their sense of wonder, thinking they have figured out how things work.

7 But the person who has achieved deep understanding becomes increasingly amazed at what they have discovered.

8 The scientist who studies the universe finds not a machine that can be completely understood but an inexhaustible mystery that reveals new layers of complexity and beauty with each advance in knowledge.

9 The person who studies human nature deeply finds not simple explanations for behavior but growing appreciation for the complexity, resilience, and creative potential of human beings.

10 This is why wonder and wisdom make such good companions—wonder motivates the search for understanding, and understanding fuels greater wonder.

8 Wonder is also connected to gratitude, though the two are different experiences that enhance each other.

2 Gratitude appreciates what you have received; wonder appreciates what you have encountered. Gratitude recognizes gifts; wonder recognizes mystery.

3 When you truly wonder at something—the intricate patterns in a leaf, the vastness of the night sky, the complexity of human emotion—gratitude naturally follows.

4 You become grateful not just for the thing itself but for your ability to perceive it, for the consciousness that allows you to be aware of beauty, for the life that makes such encounters possible.

5 Conversely, when you feel genuinely grateful for something, wonder often awakens—you begin to really see what you have been taking for granted, to notice details that appreciation brings into focus.

6 The person grateful for their health begins to wonder at the complexity of the body's systems, the precision of cellular processes, the remarkable fact that consciousness and body cooperate to create experience.

7 Together, wonder and gratitude create a powerful combination that transforms perception—wonder reveals what is worth appreciating, and gratitude motivates the attention that makes wonder possible.

8 They protect each other from distortion: wonder without gratitude can become mere intellectual curiosity disconnected from appreciation; gratitude without wonder can become routine acknowledgment that loses its transformative power.

9 The cultivation of wonder requires protecting certain mindsets that the adult world often pressures us to abandon in the name of maturity and sophistication.

2 Children naturally ask "Why?" about everything, not because they are immature but because they have not yet learned to stop questioning what they do not understand.

3 They examine simple objects with intense focus, finding endless fascination in how things feel, look, sound, and move—not because they are easily entertained but because they have not yet learned to dismiss the extraordinary as ordinary.

4 They approach new experiences with openness and curiosity rather than judging and categorizing—not because they have not yet learned to value knowing over discovering.

5 The cultivation of wonder involves recovering these qualities without losing the benefits of experience and knowledge.

6 This means learning to ask "Why?" and "How?" and "What if?" with the persistence of a child but the depth of an adult.

7 It means examining familiar things with fresh eyes while bringing mature understanding to what you observe.

8 It means approaching new experiences with openness while applying wisdom gained through previous encounters.

9 This is not regression to childhood but integration of childhood's best qualities with adulthood's genuine advantages.

10 The goal is not to become naive again but to become wise without becoming closed, knowledgeable without losing curiosity, experienced without losing the ability to be surprised.

10

Wonder also serves as protection against the spiritual deadness that can creep into life when everything becomes routine, predictable, and manageable.

2 The person who has lost their capacity for wonder begins to experience life as a series of tasks to be completed rather than mysteries to be explored, obligations to be fulfilled rather than gifts to be received.

3 They may achieve external success but find themselves feeling empty inside, going through the motions of living without feeling truly alive.

4 Wonder restores aliveness by revealing that every moment is worth exploring, every encounter offers opportunities for discovery, every day brings possibilities for surprise.

5 It reminds us that we are not just managers of our

existence but participants in an ongoing adventure whose next chapter has not yet been written.

6 The person who lives in wonder wakes up curious about what the day might bring, pays attention to the unexpected in familiar routines, remains open to learning something new even in the oldest relationships.

7 They find that wonder transforms not just perception but energy—what felt like dread becomes interesting when approached with genuine curiosity, what seemed boring becomes engaging when examined with real attention.

8 Wonder reveals that the problem was never the circumstances themselves but the way those circumstances were being approached—with assumption rather than attention, with judgment rather than curiosity, with the need to know rather than discovery.

11
There are practical ways to grow wonder that can be integrated into daily life without requiring dramatic changes in routine or circumstances.

2 Practice the art of really looking at something familiar as if seeing it for the first time. Choose one object in your daily environment—a tree outside your window, a piece of art on your wall, your own hand—and spend five minutes examining it.

3 Notice details you have never seen before. Ask questions about how it came to be this way, what forces shaped it, what story it might tell if it could speak.

4 Practice the discipline of asking "Why?" about things you normally take for granted. Why does water freeze at exactly this temperature? Why do some people's voices sound musical while others don't? Why do certain colors look beautiful together?

5 Follow these questions not to become an expert but to appreciate the complexity and mystery hidden within seemingly simple things and processes.

6 Practice engaging your senses more fully. When you eat, really taste your food. When you walk, really feel your feet touching the ground. When you listen to music, follow the melody, each harmony, each instrument.

7 Practice imagining the journey of ordinary objects. The apple you eat traveled from seed to tree to fruit to market to your kitchen. The shirt you wear was made from plants or chemicals, designed by someone, manufactured by others, transported across distances to reach you.

8 Let your imagination trace these connections, marveling at the complex web of relationships that brings even the simplest objects into your life.

9 Practice finding something new in the oldest relationships. Look for something you have never noticed before in the face of someone you see every day. Listen for inflections in their voice you have not heard. Ask them a question you have never asked.

12
As wonder becomes a regular practice rather than an occasional experience, it begins to transform not just individual moments but the entire quality of your journey as a sojourner.

2 You find yourself less concerned with controlling outcomes and more interested in discovering what wants to emerge. Less focused on getting through experiences and more engaged with fully experiencing them.

3 The awareness that your time here is limited becomes not a source of anxiety but an invitation to pay deeper attention while you can, to appreciate more fully what is available to be appreciated.

4 Wonder reveals that the journey itself is the destination —not in the sense that goals and purposes don't matter, but in the recognition that the traveling is as valuable as any arrival.

5 You begin to see that every day offers opportunities for

discovery that will never come again in exactly the same way, that every person you encounter carries mysteries worth exploring, that every moment contains depths worth appreciating.

6 This does not make you less effective or less focused but differently motivated—driven more by curiosity than by anxiety, more by appreciation than by acquisition, more by the desire to understand than by the need to control.

7 Wonder transforms problems into puzzles, obstacles into adventures, difficulties into opportunities for learning something new about creativity and the depths of your own ability.

8 It reveals that even painful experiences carry within them elements worth studying—how suffering can deepen compassion, how loss can clarify what matters most, how disappointment can redirect attention toward previously overlooked possibilities.

9 The person who lives in wonder approaches even their own death not with terror at the end of experience but with curiosity about the next mystery, the final adventure, the ultimate frontier of discovery.

10 For wonder recognizes that consciousness itself is the deepest mystery of all—this capacity to be aware, to experience, to know that you know, to love, to suffer, to hope, to dream.

11 Every moment of awareness is a miracle worth marveling at, every experience of beauty or meaning or connection a gift worth receiving with amazement.

12 In the end, wonder is not just a way of seeing but a way of being—a stance toward reality that says "Yes" to mystery, "Thank you" to beauty, "How amazing" to the simple fact of existence itself.

13 The sojourner who cultivates wonder finds that the journey, however brief, becomes not just meaningful but

magical—not in the sense of fantasy but in the deeper sense of participating consciously in the ongoing mystery of what it means to be alive, aware, and able to appreciate the gift of ordinary experience.

14 Let wonder be your companion on the path, your lens for seeing, your response to the daily miracles that surround you like air—invisible unless you pay attention, but absolutely required for the fullness of life.

$$\lim_{x \to a} f(x)$$

7

the Book of 𝕷imits

1 Consider this paradox that puzzles many sojourners: the very boundaries that seem to restrict your journey are often what make meaningful movement possible.

2 Like riverbanks that appear to confine water but actually give it direction and power, the limits you encounter in life create the channels through which your energy can flow with purpose.

3 Without riverbanks, water spreads thin across the landscape, losing its force and failing to reach its destination. Without the framework of limitations, human energy dissipates in all directions, accomplishing little and arriving nowhere.

4 Many spend their journey fighting against every

boundary they encounter, believing that freedom means the absence of all limits, not understanding that infinite possibility often leads to infinite paralysis.

5 The artist given unlimited time, unlimited resources, and unlimited canvas often creates less than the one working within the constraints of deadline, budget, and specific dimensions.

6 The student with access to all knowledge may learn less than the one focused on mastering a particular subject within a semester's time.

7 The sojourner who could go anywhere often goes nowhere, while the one with limited time and resources makes deliberate choices that create meaningful experiences.

8 Your limitations are not punishments to be endured but parameters that shape possibility, not obstacles to overcome but structures that enable creation.

9 The wise sojourner learns to work with constraints rather than against them, discovering that boundaries can become the very foundation of authentic living.

2 The first and most basic limit every sojourner faces is the boundary of time itself—your days are numbered, your years finite, your journey temporary.

2 Many see this limitation as cruel, a restriction on their ability to experience all they wish to experience, accomplish all they hope to accomplish, become all they might become.

3 Yet consider: if you had unlimited time, would any single moment carry weight? If you could delay every decision indefinitely, would any choice feel urgent enough to make?

4 The value of time comes precisely from its scarcity. The value comes today from the knowledge that it will not return. The significance of relationships deepens when you recognize they will not last forever.

5 Without the constraint of mortality, love would lack

urgency, achievement would lose meaning, and beauty would fade into the background.

6 The limitation of time forces us to prioritize—not everything can be done, so what matters most? Not every relationship can be pursued, so which ones deserve your attention? Not every opportunity can be seized, so which align with your authentic path?

7 Time's boundary creates the necessity of choice, and choice creates the possibility of meaningful direction rather than aimless wandering.

8 The person who accepts their temporal limits stops trying to do everything and starts focusing on doing the right things, stops pursuing every possibility and starts committing to particular purposes.

9 In this way, the constraint of finite time becomes not a limitation but a freedom from the impossible burden of unlimited obligations, permission to choose consciously rather than to default to unconscious choice.

3 Along with time, you face the limits of your physical abilities—your body can only be in one place, your hands can only do one task, your attention can only focus on one thing at once.

2 These physical boundaries may seem like design flaws, restrictions that prevent you from being as productive, present, or powerful as you might wish.

3 But consider the alternative: if you could be everywhere at once, would you truly be anywhere? If you could do everything simultaneously, would you do anything with excellence? If your attention could focus on all things equally, would you notice anything deeply?

4 The limitation of being in one place forces you to choose where to be, creating the possibility of being fully present rather than scattered.

5 The constraint of sequential action requires you to do one thing at a time, enabling deep engagement rather than superficiality.

6 The boundary of focused attention demands you select what deserves your attention, allowing for deep observation rather than shallow distraction.

7 Many modern sojourners exhaust themselves trying to overcome these natural limits through technology, attempting to be in multiple places virtually, multitasking their way through countless activities, dividing their attention among endless inputs.

8 But the result is often a life lived on the surface—present nowhere, great at nothing, aware of everything but understanding little.

9 The wise sojourner accepts their physical limitations as invitations to choose more purposefully, to be more present, to focus more deliberately.

10 They recognize that the power of singularity—being fully here, doing one thing completely—often accomplishes more than the illusion of multiplicity.

4 Beyond time and physical ability, you encounter the limits of your knowledge and understanding—there will always be more to learn than you can absorb, more to understand than you can grasp.

2 This intellectual boundary can feel particularly frustrating in an age where information seems limitless and answers appear to be just a search away.

3 Yet the constraint of partial knowledge serves essential purposes in the journey of wisdom.

4 If you could know everything, curiosity would die. If all mysteries were solved, wonder would disappear. If every question had an immediate answer, the joy of discovery would be lost.

5 Your limited understanding keeps you humble, preventing the arrogance that comes from believing you have mastered reality when you have only scratched its surface.

6 It keeps you open to learning, maintaining the beginner's mind that approaches each experience with fresh eyes rather than predetermined conclusions.

7 It keeps you dependent on community, requiring you to seek wisdom from others whose knowledge complements your ignorance, whose perspectives illuminate your blind spots.

8 The boundary of finite understanding also protects you from the paralysis that comes with too much information. If you had to process all possible data before making any decision, you would never act.

9 Your cognitive limits force you to work with incomplete information, developing the capacity for wise judgment rather than perfect knowledge, for reasonable faith rather than absolute certainty.

10 In this way, the boundary of limited understanding becomes not a handicap but a gift—the foundation of humility, the source of wonder, the invitation to community.

5 You also face the profound limits of your control—despite your best efforts, you cannot command outcomes, guarantee results, or determine how others will respond to your actions.

2 This boundary of influence may feel like the most restricting of all, leaving you powerless in a world where events unfold according to forces beyond your direction.

3 Yet the acceptance of limited control opens the door to a different kind of power—the power to choose your response regardless of circumstances, to maintain your integrity regardless of others' choices, to find peace regardless of outcomes.

4 When you stop exhausting yourself trying to control

what lies beyond your reach, you free enormous energy for what does remain within your influence.

5 You cannot control whether others appreciate your work, but you can control the quality of effort you bring to it.

6 You cannot control whether opportunities arise, but you can control how prepared you are when they do.

7 You cannot control how long you live, but you can control how fully you live whatever time you have.

8 The boundary of limited control forces you to focus on your response rather than others' reactions, on your choices rather than circumstances, on your character rather than your circumstances.

9 This constraint redirects your energy from external manipulation to internal growth, from trying to change the world to changing yourself, from demanding particular outcomes to committing to authentic process.

10 Paradoxically, this acceptance of limited control often increases your actual influence, as people are drawn to those who focus on their own responsibility rather than blaming external forces.

6 Perhaps the most challenging limit to accept is the boundary of your emotional capacity—you cannot feel everything deeply, care about everything equally, or maintain emotional intensity indefinitely.

2 Many sojourners believe they should be able to care about every injustice, respond to every need, and maintain constant empathy for all who suffer.

3 But emotional energy, like physical energy, is finite. The heart that tries to hold all pain breaks under the weight. The person who attempts to care about everything equally ends up caring about nothing deeply.

4 The limitation of emotional capacity requires you to choose where to invest your care, which causes deserve your

passion, which relationships merit your deepest attention.

5 This constraint protects you from being emotionally overwhelmed while enabling sustainable compassion. Better to care deeply about a few things than superficially about everything.

6 The boundary of emotional limits also creates the necessity of emotional rhythms—times of intense feeling followed by periods of rest, seasons of deep engagement alternating with intervals of restoration.

7 Just as muscles require recovery between workouts to grow stronger, emotions require rest between intensities to maintain their capacity for authentic response.

8 The wise sojourner learns to honor their emotional limits rather than ignore them, to pace their caring rather than exhaust it, to choose their battles rather than fight them all.

9 This acceptance of emotional boundaries enables sustainable engagement with life's difficulties rather than the burnout that comes from trying to feel everything all the time.

10 In this way, the limit of emotional capacity becomes not a weakness but wisdom—the foundation of enduring compassion rather than being temporarily overwhelmed.

7 Your energy itself is perhaps your most precious limited resource—not just physical energy but the overall energy that fuels your engagement with life.

2 Every day you wake with a certain amount of energy to spend, and every choice you make either depletes or restores this limited resource.

3 Many sojourners spend their energy unconsciously, like someone shopping without checking their account balance, only discovering their lack of funds when it is too late.

4 They say yes to every request, pursue every opportunity, and maintain every relationship without considering the energetic cost of their commitments.

5 But wise sojourners understand that energy is a limited resource that must be spent with purpose rather than wasted carelessly.

6 They learn to ask not just "Can I do this?" but "Is this the best use of my limited energy? Will this expense serve my authentic path or merely fill time?"

7 Some activities drain energy while giving little in return—relationships that demand constant maintenance without offering growth, work that depletes energy without creating meaning, commitments that consume time without serving a purpose.

8 Other activities restore more energy than they require—relationships that nourish rather than drain, work that energizes rather than exhausts, commitments that align with rather than contradict your authentic self.

9 The constraint of limited energy forces you to become conscious about where you invest your vitality, leading to choices that sustain rather than deplete your capacity for engagement.

10 When you treat energy as a limited currency rather than unlimited resource, you begin spending it on what matters most rather than what demands loudest.

8 The limits you face are not equally restrictive—some boundaries confine while others define, some constraints diminish while others focus.

2 Learning the difference between helpful and harmful limits becomes necessary wisdom for navigating your temporary journey.

3 Helpful limits provide structure that enables rather than prevents authentic living. Like the banks of a river that give water direction and power, these boundaries channel your energy toward meaningful destinations.

4 Harmful limits, however, artificially restrict your

authentic development, like dams that stop the natural flow of water. These constraints may serve others' interests while limiting your genuine growth.

5 The deadline that motivates you to complete important work serves as helpful limitation.

6 The perfectionism that prevents you from ever finishing anything functions as harmful constraint.

7 The budget that forces you to choose priorities creates helpful boundaries. The scarcity mindset that prevents you from investing in growth imposes harmful restrictions.

8 The relationship boundaries that protect your energy enable authentic connection. The fear-based walls that prevent all vulnerability create harmful isolation.

9 Wise sojourners learn to embrace helpful limits while challenging harmful ones, to work within constructive constraints while removing destructive restrictions.

10 This requires skill to distinguish between the two, courage to accept necessary boundaries, and determination to break free from artificial limitations.

11 The goal is not to eliminate all limits but to align yourself with limitations that serve your authentic development while releasing constraints that prevent your genuine growth.

9 When you truly accept your basic limitations, something remarkable happens—instead of feeling constrained, you begin to feel liberated.

2 The acceptance of finite time frees you from the impossible burden of trying to do everything, allowing you to focus on what matters most.

3 The acknowledgment of limited knowledge releases you from the pressure to have all answers, permitting you to live comfortably with questions and uncertainty.

4 The recognition of restricted control delivers you from the

exhausting effort to control outcomes beyond your influence, enabling you to focus on what you can actually change.

5 The understanding of bounded energy empowers you to spend your energy consciously rather than depleting it unconsciously through poor choices.

6 This liberation through limitation creates space for authentic living—not life as you imagine it should be with unlimited resources, but life as it actually is within real constraints.

7 The person who accepts their limits stops wasting energy fighting reality and starts using that energy to work creatively within reality's boundaries.

8 They discover that constraints can spark innovation, that boundaries can inspire creativity, that limitations can generate focus.

9 The artist working within the constraint of specific materials often creates more interesting work than one with unlimited supplies. The poet working within the limits of sonnets often achieves greater beauty than one with no formal restrictions.

10 Similarly, the life lived within accepted limitations often achieves greater depth, meaning, and satisfaction than the life spent fighting against all constraints.

10 The ultimate wisdom about limits is recognizing that they are not barriers to authentic living but the very conditions that make authentic living possible.

2 Without the constraint of time, nothing would be valuable. Without the limitation of space, nowhere would be special. Without the boundary of mortality, life would lack urgency and meaning.

3 Your limits do not prevent you from becoming who you are meant to be—they are part of what shapes who you can become.

4 The river does not fight against its banks but uses them to flow with power toward its destination. The tree does not resent the constraint of gravity but uses it to grow deep roots and reach great heights.

5 Similarly, the wise sojourner does not waste energy battling against the basic constraints of human existence but learns to work within them, discovering that limitations often become the very source of creative power.

6 Your temporariness is not your enemy but your teacher, not your prison but your palette, not your weakness but your wisdom.

7 When you embrace your limits rather than fight them, accept your boundaries rather than ignore them, work with your constraints rather than against them, you discover a form of freedom that those who deny limitations never know.

8 This is the freedom of focus over scattered attention, depth over breadth, quality over quantity, presence over absence.

9 It is the freedom of choosing consciously within real constraints rather than choosing unconsciously while pretending constraints don't exist.

10 It is the freedom of being fully human—limited, finite, temporary—rather than the exhaustion of trying to be something you were never designed to be.

11

As you learn to work creatively within your limitations, you begin to see them not as problems to solve but as features that enable rather than prevent meaningful living.

2 The constraint of needing sleep creates rhythms of rest and activity that allow for both engagement and restoration.

3 The limitation of needing food creates opportunities for conversation, and celebration through shared meals.

4 The boundary of needing shelter creates spaces for intimacy, privacy, and belonging.

5 The restriction of needing relationships creates bonds that provide meaning, support, and love.

6 Every human limitation creates corresponding human possibilities. Every constraint opens different pathways of experience. Every boundary enables particular forms of growth.

7 The key is learning to see limitations as doorways rather than walls, as invitations rather than restrictions, as opportunities rather than obstacles.

8 When faced with a constraint, the wise sojourner asks not "How can I get rid of this limitation?" but "How can I work creatively within it? What possibilities does this boundary create? What might I discover by accepting rather than fighting this constraint?"

9 This shift in perspective changes the entire experience of limitation from frustration to fascination, from resentment to acceptance, from fighting to flowing.

10 You begin to see your life not as a series of restrictions to overcome but as a unique frame within which to create something beautiful, meaningful, and authentically yours.

12 In the end, the deepest wisdom about limits is this: your limits are not arbitrary punishments but necessary conditions for the particular form of beauty your life is meant to create.

2 Just as every work of art achieves its beauty through working within certain limitations—the painter within the boundary of canvas, the musician within the structure of scales, the poet within the constraints of language—your life achieves its unique beauty by working creatively within its particular limitations.

3 The limits you face are not the same as those faced by any other sojourner. Your particular combination of time, energy, capacity, and circumstance creates a unique framework within which only you can create the masterpiece of your existence.

4 To spend your journey fighting against these limitations is to waste the very conditions that make your particular form of beauty possible.

5 To accept and work within your constraints is to partner with reality in creating something that could never exist without exactly these boundaries, exactly these parameters, exactly these conditions.

6 Your limitations are not flaws in your design but features that enable your unique contribution to the human experience.

7 The note you are meant to play in the great composition of existence can only be played within the constraints of your particular instrument, in the key of your particular circumstances, with the timing of your particular moment.

8 Embrace your limits as the sacred boundaries that make your authentic life possible.

9 Work within them as the creative constraints that enable your unique expression.

10 For in learning to live fully within your limitations, you discover not confinement but freedom—the freedom to be completely, authentically, beautifully you.

11 This is the paradox and the gift of finite existence: that by accepting what you cannot do, you discover what you can do; by embracing what you cannot be, you become who you are meant to be; by working within your limitations, you transcend them in the most profound way possible—through the creation of a life that is entirely, uniquely, authentically yours.

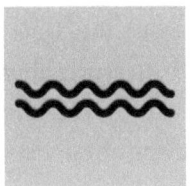

8
the Book of Tides

1 Consider how our journey through this world unfolds not along a straight and unchanging path, but through landscapes of constant change.

2 For the Creator has established a rhythm, a pattern of seasons, opposing yet complementary forces. This is the basic nature of existence that the wise sojourner comes to recognize and accept.

3 Look at the heavens and the earth: day follows night, and night follows day. Summer gives way to autumn, autumn to winter, winter to spring, and spring once more to summer. The tide comes in and goes out, the moon grows full and then wanes, stars rise and set.

4 So too in our lives do we find these natural pairs: times

of plenty and times of little, periods of health and times of illness, moments of clarity and moments of confusion, days of connection and nights of solitude.

5 These opposites are not flaws in creation's design but essential parts of its pattern. Without darkness, how would we understand light? Without cold, how would we know warmth? Without hunger, how would we appreciate food? Without parting, how would we value reunion?

6 Many sojourners resist this basic truth. They try to live permanently in a land of pleasure, abundance, health, and joy. They build homes meant to shield them from pain, loss, illness, and sorrow, believing these experiences to be mistakes in the journey rather than important parts of the path.

7 Others give in to fatalism, believing themselves helpless before these changing times. When darkness comes, they lose faith in the return of light. When winter blows in, they forget the promise of spring. They see only the present condition, blind to the larger pattern.

8 The wise sojourner takes neither approach, instead developing the ability to recognize and navigate these natural pairs with both awareness and acceptance. They neither deny the reality of opposing forces nor let themselves be defined by any single experience within the greater flow.

2 Of all the pairs the sojourner faces, none is more profound than that between life and death. From the first breath drawn at birth to the final breath released at departure, we exist in relationship to this fundamental pairing.

2 Life without awareness of death becomes shallow, its moments taken for granted, its gifts received without wonder.

3 Death without understanding of life becomes only an ending, its meaning diminished, its approach met only with fear.

4 The wise sojourner sees how life and death dance

together at every moment of the journey. In each breath, air is breathed in and released. In each step, weight is gained and surrendered. Within each day, waking gives way to sleep. In each task, beginning moves toward completion.

5 Consider how the seed must cease to be a seed to become a plant. Consider how the caterpillar must surrender its form to become a butterfly. Consider how the day must die for the stars to become visible. Consider how the field must be cleared for new growth.

6 Death is not merely the end of the journey but a presence that travels alongside us, not as enemy but as teacher - reminding us of our limited time, sharpening our appreciation for passing beauty, clarifying what truly matters on the path.

7 The sojourner who acknowledges death's companionship lives differently—more fully present, more deeply grateful, more intentional in choices, more authentic in connections. Not morbid in obsession with endings, but alive in awareness of precious moments.

8 For our path does not truly begin at birth and end at death, but participates in a greater cycle that began before our arrival and continues beyond our departure.

9 Individual journeys form threads in a vast tapestry whose full pattern no single sojourner can see.

10 Therefore, let us neither cling desperately to life nor surrender prematurely to death, but walk in a conscious relationship with both—honoring life through full participation and respecting death through humble acceptance.

3 Along our path come seasons of joy and periods of sorrow, neither of which remains permanently. Like sojourners themselves, these emotions visit for a time and then depart, making way for new experiences.

2 Many seek to dwell exclusively in the lands of joy,

celebration, and pleasure, viewing sorrow, grief, and pain as intruders to be removed from their journey.

3 They pursue happiness as though it were a permanent destination rather than a recurring visitor.

4 Others become so accustomed to sorrow's landscape that they grow suspicious of joy when it appears, believing it merely leads to disappointment, a momentary relief before the inevitable return to suffering.

5 They brace themselves against happiness to avoid the pain of its departure.

6 The wise sojourner understands that joy and sorrow are not separate but interconnected. The ability to feel one is linked with the ability to experience the other. They mirror each other.

7 Consider how a parent's joy in their child arises from the same love that makes possible their grief at separation.

8 Consider how reunion's joy is proportional to absence's pain.

9 Joy without the context of sorrow becomes a shallow, momentary distraction without depth or meaning.

10 Sorrow without the memory of joy becomes despair, a darkness that forgets the existence of light.

11 The sojourner who has walked through valleys of grief discovers unexpected treasures not found on the mountaintops: deeper compassion for fellow sojourners, greater appreciation when joy returns, increased ability to sit with others in their pain without needing to fix or run.

12 Those who have experienced the mountaintops of joy carry that light with them even into the shadows, not as denial of the present darkness but as knowledge that the landscape will change again, that dawn follows even the longest night.

13 Therefore, let us welcome both joy and sorrow as teachers on the path, neither clinging to one nor rejecting the other.

4 We travel through seasons of health and periods of pain, weakness, and illness. The body that carries us through the journey knows both strength and weakness.

2 In times of health, many sojourners forget their body's wisdom and limits. They treat it as a possession to be used rather than a companion to be honored. They take for granted its intricateness until disruption reminds them of its complexity.

3 In times of illness or pain, many identify with their suffering, seeing it as the whole of who they are rather than a temporary condition through which they are passing. They lose sight of the greater journey beyond the present difficulty.

4 The wise sojourner relates to the body with neither neglect nor obsession, neither reckless disregard nor anxious monitoring.

5 When health abounds, they receive it with gratitude rather than entitlement, using their strength to fulfill their purpose and support others, knowing that life is both a gift and responsibility.

6 When illness or pain arrives, they neither deny its reality nor give it authority. They listen to what it may teach—about limits, priorities, interdependence, and the distinction between what can be changed and what must be accepted.

7 The body's alternating experiences of pleasure and pain, ease and struggle, wellness and sickness create a wisdom not available through theoretical understanding. We learn through direct experience what no teaching alone can expound.

8 For the body carries within it the essential pairs of existence—it is both remarkably strong and inherently weak, both intricately unique and fundamentally common.

9 Therefore, let us honor our physical vessel throughout its changing conditions, treating it neither as ultimate identity nor as irrelevant container, but as essential companion designed for a journey of both limitation and extraordinary.

5 We walk a path where knowledge and mystery continually interact, where understanding enlightens portions of the journey while vast expanses remain shrouded in questions beyond answering.

2 Some sojourners seek certainty above all, collecting facts and explanations as though complete knowledge were possible, as though the correct map might finally eliminate all lostness. They mistake the models they create for the land itself.

3 Others surrender to confusion, believing that because complete understanding is impossible, the pursuit of knowledge is pointless. They drift without direction, making no effort to light the path before them, resigned to confusion.

4 The wise sojourner understands that knowledge and mystery are not opponents but partners in the journey.

5 What we know are like islands in a vast sea of what we do not know.

6 Consider how each discovery reveals new questions. Consider how deeper understanding often increases awareness of greater complexity. Consider how the most profound knowledge frequently begins with recognition of ignorance.

7 The sojourner who honors both knowledge and mystery journeys with both map and compass. The map represents what others have discovered and shared—the accumulated wisdom of fellow sojourners. The compass represents inner guidance for when the land doesn't match available maps.

8 This balanced approach allows us to navigate through both charted and uncharted lands. When existing knowledge serves, the sojourner gratefully follows established roads. When mysteries arise beyond current understanding, they proceed with humble curiosity rather than frustrated resistance.

9 For the most magnificent views often appear at the

boundary between the known and unknown, where wonder and wisdom meet, where understanding provides the foundation for exploring what lies beyond current knowledge.

10 Therefore, let us pursue knowledge without demanding certainty, seek understanding without requiring complete explanation, and embrace mystery without surrendering to confusion. Herein lies both intellectual integrity and spiritual openness.

6 We experience both deep connection with fellow sojourners and profound solitude on the path. These contrasting yet complementary states form the rhythm of relationships that sustains the journey.

2 Some seek constant companionship, filling every moment with interaction, conversation, and shared experience. They fear silence and aloneness, believing meaning exists only in connection with others, defining themselves entirely through relationships.

3 Others isolate themselves from meaningful engagement, believing self-sufficiency is the highest virtue, vulnerability the greatest risk, independence the surest protection. They maintain distance even when physically present, revealing little of their true selves.

4 The wise sojourner recognizes that human growth requires both—genuine connection for food for thought and meaningful solitude for restoration. Each prepares the way for the other in an ongoing cycle of engagement and reflection.

5 In connection, we discover aspects of ourselves that are invisible when alone, receive perspectives beyond our limited viewpoint, experience the healing power of being truly seen and accepted, and participate in purposes larger than individual meaning alone.

6 In solitude, we integrate experiences, listen to inner wisdom often drowned out by external voices, reconnect with

our authentic path rather than following others' expectations, and grow self-knowledge necessary for genuine relationships.

7 These alternating experiences are not contradictory but complementary. Rich connection becomes possible because of the grounded sense of self developed in solitude. Meaningful solitude becomes possible because of the security and affirmation received in connection.

8 Therefore, let us embrace both the coming together and the pulling apart, neither clinging to others out of fear nor isolating out of self-protection, but moving with the natural rhythm of community and contemplation that sustains the soul's journey.

7 Having recognized these fundamental pairs, how shall we navigate our journey?

2 Not by seeking perfect balance, as though life could be controlled, but by developing the ability to move with the natural rhythms of existence.

3 The sojourner who recognizes the larger rhythm experiences current conditions differently—seeing them not as permanent states but as passing seasons, not as final destinations but as lands being explored.

4 In times of plenty, they do not assume endless prosperity but prepare for leaner times. In times of scarcity, they do not despair but remember previous provisions and maintain faith in future restoration.

5 They read the landscape with perspective beyond the immediate.

6 The rigid sojourner breaks under changing conditions; the adaptable one bends and continues.

7 The sojourner who expects consistency meets disappointment; the one who anticipates change finds resilience.

8 Like a sailor skilled in reading winds and currents, the

wise sojourner learns to adjust their approach according to present conditions—sometimes moving with focused intensity, sometimes pausing for healing, sometimes changing direction when the path requires.

9 Spring is for planting, summer for growing, autumn for harvesting, winter for resting. Each serves the greater cycle, each plays its essential role. So too do the varying conditions of our journey serve purposes within the larger pattern.

10 Times of joy naturally expand capacity for appreciation and connection.

11 Times of sorrow deepen compassion and perspective.

12 Times of clarity enable decisive action.

13 Times of confusion foster humility and openness.

14 We can trust in coming change without demanding its immediate arrival. We can be aware of the larger pattern without rejecting the present experience. We can live simultaneously with acceptance of what is and faith in what shall be.

15 This is not passive resignation but active engagement with the fullness of life. Not detachment from reality but deeper immersion in its complete nature. Not denial of difficulty but placing it within a greater truth of ongoing change and growth.

16 The sojourner who learns to live within these rhythms discovers a peace that surpasses circumstances—not because all experiences are pleasant, but because all are recognized as parts of a journey whose ultimate direction moves toward integration rather than fragmentation, toward wholeness rather than division.

17 Though the path winds through the valleys and over the mountains, through fertile plains and empty deserts, through populated towns and solitary wilderness, it remains a single journey guided by wisdom beyond our comprehension but not beyond our growing trust.

18 Therefore, let us travel with both awareness of life's contrasts and confidence in its underlying meaning.

19 Let us embrace each season for its particular gifts while holding to the knowledge of the greater cycle.

20 Let us face each day's reality while maintaining vision of the journey's bigger story.

21 For in this way, we live with eyes both open to present and lifted toward the future, with heart both honest about current feelings and anchored in a deeper truth, with hands both engaged in immediate tasks and extended for eternal purposes.

22 This is the way of the wise sojourner—to navigate life's pairs not by seeking impossible balance but by moving in harmony with their natural rhythm, finding in their very alternation not contradiction but completion, not confusion but clarity, not chaos but order.

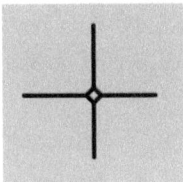

9

the Book of Seasons

1 Think about how the sojourner journeys not through a single unchanging landscape, but through distinct territories, each with its own climate, customs, and character.

2 Just as the earth moves through spring, summer, autumn, and winter in an endless cycle, so too does the human journey unfold through seasons of life, each bringing its own gifts, challenges, and wisdom.

3 Many people resist these natural transitions, trying to remain permanently in the season they find most comfortable, like someone attempting to hold back winter by refusing to acknowledge that autumn has ended.

4 Others rush impatiently through their current season, always looking ahead to the next phase, like sojourners so

focused on their destination that they miss the beauty of the landscape they're passing through.

5 But the wise sojourner understands that each season of life is a distinct country to be fully explored, with its own treasures to discover and lessons to learn.

6 Childhood is the land of wonder, where everything is new and possible. Youth is the territory of exploration, where energy meets opportunity. Midlife is the region of responsibility and harvest, where seeds planted earlier bear fruit. Elderhood is the realm of wisdom, where experience becomes legacy.

7 Each season builds upon the previous one while preparing for the next, like chapters in a book that are different yet connected, each contributing to the complete story of a life.

8 The person who tries to skip seasons or remain in them beyond their time finds themselves out of harmony with the natural rhythm of growth and change that governs all living things.

9 For we are not meant to be perpetual children, eternal youth, or unchanging adults. We are meant to be sojourners moving through the full spectrum of human experience, gathering the unique gifts each season offers.

2 Childhood is the springtime of life, when everything is fresh, new, and full of possibility.

2 In this season, the sojourner dwells in the present moment with an intensity that adults often envy. The child does not worry about tomorrow's weather or regret yesterday's mistakes—they are fully alive to the wonder of now.

3 This is the time of rapid growth, when the body reaches toward its full height and the mind absorbs knowledge.

4 Everything is a first experience: the first taste of ice

cream, the first sight of the ocean, the first understanding of friendship, the first encounter with loss.

5 In childhood, play is work and work is play. Learning happens through exploration, through touching and tasting and experimenting with the world.

6 The child's questions are profound in their simplicity: "Why is the sky blue? Where do people go when they die? Why do grown-ups cry?" They ask without embarrassment what adults have learned to accept without understanding.

7 Childhood gifts the sojourner with imagination that can transform a cardboard box into a spaceship, with trust that believes adults when they say everything will be okay, with toughness that bounces back from disappointment with surprising speed.

8 Childhood also brings the security of being cared for by others, of having needs met without having to earn that care, of belonging to a family or community simply by existing.

9 Yet this season also includes the gradual discovery that the world contains both beauty and pain, that not all adults can be trusted, that fairness is an ideal rather than a guarantee.

10 The wise adult remembers the gifts of childhood without romanticizing its limitations, carrying forward the wonder and openness while leaving behind the dependency and naivety.

3 Youth is the summer of life, when energy burns bright and the horizon beckons with infinite possibility.

2 This is the season of becoming, when the sojourner begins to discover who they might be beyond the identity given to them by family and circumstance.

3 The body reaches its pinnacle of strength and beauty, capable of efforts that will seem impossible in later seasons. The mind is quick and sharp, able to absorb new information and master new skills with remarkable speed.

4 Youth is the time of first independence, when the sojourner begins to make their own choices about relationships, career, values, and direction in life.

5 Everything feels urgent and immediate. Love burns with passionate intensity. Causes are worth fighting for. Dreams seem not just possible but certain.

6 This is the season of exploration and experimentation, when the sojourner tests boundaries, challenges authority, and discovers the consequences of their own choices.

7 Youth brings the gift of idealism—the belief that the world can and should be better, that problems can be solved, that positive change is not only possible but necessary.

8 It offers the courage of inexperience, the willingness to attempt what older, wiser people know is difficult or unlikely to succeed.

9 Yet youth also brings the burden of choice without the wisdom of experience. The young sojourner must make important decisions about education, career, and relationships with limited knowledge of their long-term consequences.

10 This season often includes mistakes—sometimes painful ones—that no classroom can provide.

11 The anxiety of youth comes from having endless possibilities but needing to choose among them, from wanting to experience everything but having time for only a fraction of what the world offers.

12 The wise sojourner looks back on youth with gratitude for its energy and passion while recognizing that its very limitations were part of what made its gifts possible.

4 Midlife is the autumn of life, when the sojourner reaps what they have sown and begins to understand the weight of their choices.

2 This is the season of responsibility, when others depend on the sojourner's strength, wisdom, and resources. Children

need to be raised, elderly parents may need care, communities require leadership.

3 The body begins to show signs of wear, reminding the sojourner that their time and energy are finite resources that must be managed rather than spent freely.

4 This is when earlier dreams either come to fruition or need revision. The career path either leads where hoped or requires redirection. Relationships either deepen into lasting partnership or reveal their limitations.

5 Midlife brings the gift of competence—skills developed through years of practice, knowledge gained through experience, confidence earned through both success and failure.

6 It offers the satisfaction of building something lasting—a family, a career, a contribution to community that extends beyond personal benefit.

7 This season provides the perspective that comes from having lived long enough to see patterns, to understand consequences, to recognize what matters and what doesn't.

8 Yet midlife also brings the awareness of mortality that was abstract in youth. Parents die, friends face serious illness, the body shows signs of aging. The sojourner realizes they have likely lived more years than they have ahead of them.

9 This recognition can trigger what is often called a "midlife crisis"—the urgent desire to recapture youth, to pursue delayed dreams, to make radical changes before it's too late.

10 The wise sojourner navigates this season by accepting rather than fighting its realities, by finding new forms of vitality rather than trying to recapture old ones.

11 They understand that midlife's limitations are balanced by its freedoms—freedom from the uncertainty of youth, freedom to apply hard-won wisdom, freedom to focus on what truly matters.

12 This is the season when the sojourner can be most useful to others, combining the energy of youth with the wisdom of experience.

5 Elderhood is the winter of life, when the sojourner's role shifts from building to sharing, from acquiring to giving away, from doing to being.

2 This is the season of reflection, when the long view of life becomes possible, when patterns that were invisible up close become clear from the perspective of years.

3 The body may weaken, but the spirit often grows stronger. What is lost in physical capability is often gained in emotional strength and spiritual depth.

4 Elderhood brings the gift of wisdom—not just knowledge, but understanding; not just information, but insight into what knowledge means and how it applies to the art of living well.

5 This season offers the freedom that comes from having already proven yourself, from no longer needing to establish your worth or build your reputation.

6 The elder sojourner can speak truth without worrying about career consequences, can take risks that younger people cannot afford, can focus on legacy rather than advancement.

7 This is the time when stories become important—not just personal stories, but the larger story of which the individual life has been a part.

8 Elderhood provides perspective on what endures and what passes away, what was worth the investment of time and energy and what was not.

9 Yet this season also brings losses—the death of peers, the decline of physical abilities, the awareness that time is running short.

10 The challenge of elderhood is to face these realities with grace rather than bitterness, to find meaning in decline, to

discover new forms of purpose when old ones are no longer possible.

11 The wise elder learns to let go gracefully—of roles that defined them, of physical capabilities they once took for granted, of control over outcomes they cannot influence.

12 They find their value not in what they can still do but in what they have learned, not in their productivity but in their presence.

13 Elderhood offers the unique gift of being able to see the whole arc of life, to understand how seemingly disconnected events actually formed a coherent pattern.

14 This perspective allows elders to offer younger sojourners something invaluable: the assurance that the journey has meaning even when individual steps seem random or pointless.

6 The transition between seasons is often the most challenging part of the journey, as the sojourner must leave behind familiar territory and venture into unknown landscape.

2 Moving from childhood to youth requires releasing the security of being cared for by others and accepting the responsibility of making your own choices.

3 Many struggle with this transition, either clinging to dependency longer than healthy or rushing toward independence before they have developed the wisdom to handle it well.

4 The shift from youth to midlife demands trading possibilities for choices, acknowledging that choosing one path means not choosing others.

5 This can feel like loss—the death of dreams, the closing of doors, the recognition that life is more limited than youth imagined.

6 The passage from midlife to elderhood requires accepting decline after a lifetime of growth, finding new

sources of meaning when familiar ones are no longer available.

7 Each transition asks the sojourner to release what they have outgrown while embracing what they are becoming, to honor what was while opening to what could be.

8 The difficulty of transitions often comes from trying to bring the habits, expectations, and strategies of one season into another where they no longer fit.

9 The young person who tries to maintain the carefree attitude of childhood struggles with the responsibilities of adult life.

10 The middle-aged person who attempts to live with the intensity and risk-taking of youth exhausts themselves and neglects their obligations.

11 The elder who cannot release the need for control and productivity that served them in midlife misses the gifts that elderhood offers.

12 Graceful transition requires recognizing when a season is ending and allowing it to end, grieving what is lost while opening to what is gained.

7 The art of transitioning well between seasons begins with accepting that change is natural and necessary, not a failure or betrayal of what came before.

2 Like trees that must release their leaves in autumn to survive the winter, humans must sometimes let go of what once gave them life in order to continue growing.

3 This requires the courage to live in the uncertainty between seasons—no longer what you were, not yet what you will become.

4 During these transitional times, the sojourner may feel lost, confused, or anxious about their identity and direction.

5 The wise response is to lean into this uncertainty rather than fighting it, to see transition as a creative space rather than an empty void.

6 Just as winter appears dead but is actually a time of hidden preparation for spring's renewal, life transitions often contain invisible growth that only becomes apparent later.

7 Navigating transition well requires both looking back with gratitude and looking forward with hope, honoring what has been while remaining open to what might be.

8 It means seeking guidance from those who have successfully made similar transitions while recognizing that your particular journey will be unique.

9 Transition is often a time for ritual and ceremony—formal ways of marking the end of one phase and the beginning of another.

10 These markers help both the individual and their community recognize and honor the significance of the change taking place.

11 Whether it's a graduation, a wedding, a retirement party, or a more personal ritual of your own creation, ceremony provides structure for what can otherwise feel chaotic.

12 Most importantly, successful transition requires patience with the process and trust that the next season will bring its own gifts, even if they are different from what you expected or hoped for.

8 To live fully in each season requires understanding and embracing its unique gifts rather than wishing you were in a different phase of life.

2 The child who tries to act like an adult misses the wonder and play that are childhood's special treasures.

3 The adult who tries to recreate their youth wastes the competence and wisdom that are midlife's particular offerings.

4 Each season has its own forms of beauty, its own opportunities for growth, its own contributions to make to the complete symphony of a life.

5 Living fully in your current season means accepting its limitations while maximizing its possibilities.

6 The young person can't have the wisdom of age, but they can have the energy and optimism that age often lacks.

7 The elder can't have the physical strength of youth, but they can have the perspective and freedom that youth hasn't yet earned.

8 Rather than envying other seasons, the wise sojourner asks: "What can only be done well in this particular phase of life? What opportunities are uniquely available to me now?"

9 This might mean embracing the adventure and risk-taking that youth allows, the building and achieving that midlife enables, or the teaching and legacy-creating that elderhood makes possible.

10 Living fully in your season also means preparing wisely for the next one without becoming so future-focused that you miss the present.

11 The young person who develops good habits and strong relationships creates a foundation for a healthy midlife.

12 The middle-aged person who maintains their health and continues learning prepares for an engaged and vital elderhood.

13 The elder who shares their wisdom and tends to their relationships leaves a legacy that continues beyond their own season.

14 But this preparation should enhance rather than replace full engagement with current opportunities and responsibilities.

9 One of the great gifts of understanding life's seasons is the perspective it provides on temporary difficulties and phases that feel permanent.

2 The struggling student can take comfort in knowing that

the challenges of learning are concentrated in youth and will ease with time.

3 The overwhelmed parent can remember that the intensity of child-rearing is a phase, not a permanent condition.

4 The elder facing physical decline can focus on the spiritual and relational opportunities that this season uniquely provides.

5 Understanding seasons also helps us appreciate people in different phases of life rather than judging them by the standards of our own season.

6 The adult can admire the energy and idealism of youth without dismissing it as naive.

7 The young person can respect the caution and experience of elders without seeing it as timidity.

8 Each season needs the others—youth needs the guidance of experience, midlife needs the energy of youth and the wisdom of elders, elderhood needs the vitality of younger generations to carry forward what they have built.

9 A healthy community includes people in all seasons of life, each contributing their unique gifts while learning from those in other phases.

10 The teenager's passion for justice energizes the adult's practical efforts for change while being tempered by the elder's understanding of complexity.

11 The elder's long view balances the middle-aged person's urgency while being renewed by contact with youth's hope.

12 In this way, the seasons of individual lives interweave to create the larger seasons of community and culture.

10 Perhaps the deepest wisdom about life's seasons is this: each phase is both a destination and a journey, complete in itself yet part of something larger.

2 Childhood is not just preparation for youth; it is childhood—valuable and meaningful in its own right.

3 Youth is not merely a stepping stone to adulthood; it has its own gifts and purposes that cannot be replicated in any other season.

4 Midlife is not simply a bridge between youth and age; it offers experiences and opportunities available nowhere else in the human journey.

5 Elderhood is not a consolation prize for surviving the other seasons; it provides wisdom and perspective that are its own unique treasures.

6 This understanding frees us from the tyranny of thinking that one season is inherently better than others, that the goal is to reach a particular phase and stay there.

7 Instead, we can embrace the full arc of human experience, recognizing that each season serves the whole while being valuable in itself.

8 The greatest tragedy is not aging or dying, but failing to fully inhabit whichever season you find yourself in.

9 Whether you are in the spring of childhood, the summer of youth, the autumn of midlife, or the winter of elderhood, this is your time.

10 This season has gifts for you to receive and gifts for you to give that are available only now, in this particular phase of your journey.

11 Do not spend your childhood wishing to be grown up, your youth planning for middle age, your midlife dreading elderhood, or your elderhood regretting the past.

12 Each season will come and go in its own time. Your task is to be fully present to the one you are currently traveling through.

13 For in the end, a life well-lived is not one that stayed forever young or reached a perfect destination, but one that experienced the full journey with all its seasons—each phase

embraced, explored, and appreciated for its unique contribution to the complete story of a human life.

14 The seasons teach us that change is not the enemy of meaning but its partner, that growth requires both holding on and letting go, that the beauty of life lies not in any single moment but in the full cycle of moments that make up the extraordinary journey from beginning to end.

10

the Book of Work

1 Consider how much of your brief journey is spent in labor—the daily effort to provide for yourself and others, to contribute to the world of work, to focus your abilities into useful purpose.

2 From your first childhood chores to the projects of your later years, work shapes the rhythm of your days and the direction of your path.

3 Yet many sojourners misunderstand the role of work in their sojourn, treating it either as the whole purpose of life or as a burden to be endured until escape becomes possible.

4 Some build their entire identity around their occupation, saying "I am a teacher" or "I am a lawyer" instead of "I teach" or "I practice law."

5 When their career ends through retirement, illness, or change of circumstances, they feel they have lost not just their job but themselves, as if their worth were measured entirely by their productive output.

6 Others treat work as mere drudgery, counting hours until quitting time, days until weekend, years until retirement, viewing labor as the price paid for the privilege of truly living during off-hours.

7 They divide life into work-time and real-time, seeing employment as theft of their authentic existence rather than expression of it.

8 But there is a wiser way to understand work during your temporary stay here—not as your ultimate identity nor as meaningless toil, but as temporary stewardship of tasks that serve the greater human good.

9 For the work you do is not truly yours—it existed before you arrived and will continue after you depart. You are its caretaker for a season, responsible for advancing it while you can, then passing it along to others.

2 Understanding work as stewardship rather than ownership changes everything about how you approach your daily labor.

2 The farmer who sees herself as temporary steward of the land works differently than one who sees the farm as permanent possession—with greater respect for the soil's long-term health, deeper appreciation for its productive capacity, clearer understanding of her role in the longer story of cultivation.

3 The teacher who understands his classroom is temporary approaches education differently than one who sees students as his to control—with humility about what he can accomplish in a limited time, gratitude for the opportunity to influence young minds, recognition that learning continues long after his direct involvement ends.

4 When you see your work as stewardship, you no longer carry the burden of believing you must accomplish everything, solve every problem, or leave your field perfect.

5 Your responsibility is to tend faithfully what has been entrusted to you, to improve what you can during your time of service, and to prepare the way for those who will follow.

6 This perspective relieves the anxiety that comes from treating career success as the measure of a life's worth while maintaining the dignity that comes from meaningful contribution.

7 You work with purpose but without desperation, with commitment but without obsession, with excellence but without perfectionism.

8 For you understand that your role, however important, is temporary—you are playing a part in a much larger story, writing lines to a novel you did not begin and will not complete.

3 The sojourner's perspective on work recognizes that all honest labor has dignity, regardless of how society ranks different occupations in its hierarchies of prestige and compensation.

2 The janitor who maintains clean spaces serves human growth as truly as the executive who makes strategic decisions. The farmer who grows food contributes to civilization as meaningfully as the professor who advances knowledge.

3 Each form of work addresses real human needs—for order, for nourishment, for learning, for healing, for beauty, for connection, for safety, for meaning.

4 When your time here is understood as limited, the question becomes not "What work will make me most important?" but "How can I best serve during my brief opportunity to contribute?"

5 This shift in perspective can transform even routine

labor into meaningful service when you recognize its place in the web of work that sustains humanity and its communities.

6 The person who stocks shelves in a grocery store enables families to feed themselves. The one who answers phones in a customer service center helps solve problems that matter to real people. The individual who cleans office buildings creates environments where others can focus on their contributions.

7 No work done with integrity and care is beneath dignity when understood as temporary stewardship of humanity's ongoing project of creating conditions for growth.

8 Your work may seem small in the grand scheme of things, but the grand scheme is made up entirely of seemingly small contributions working together.

9 The awareness that your time is limited makes clear that wasting it on work that truly serves no good purpose—that harms rather than helps, that destroys rather than builds—is poor stewardship of your temporary ability to contribute.

4 Many sojourners confuse career with calling, thinking these terms describe the same reality, not understanding the profound difference between them.

2 Career is the sequence of jobs and positions that provide your livelihood, the external progression of roles and responsibilities that others can observe and measure.

3 Calling is the deeper purpose that motivates your work, the sense of direction that gives meaning to your labor, the conviction that your efforts serve something worthy of your brief time here.

4 Career is about advancement—moving up ladders, gaining titles, increasing compensation, accumulating achievements that others recognize.

5 Calling is about contribution—using your gifts to serve needs larger than your own, finding ways to participate

meaningfully in the work of healing, building, creating, teaching, protecting, or nurturing.

6 You can have a successful career without a clear calling, climbing professionally while feeling spiritually empty about the purpose of your work.

7 You can also pursue a calling that never becomes a traditional career, finding your deepest purpose in volunteer work, family care, community service, or creative endeavors that provide little external recognition or financial reward.

8 The fortunate sojourner discovers ways to align career and calling, finding paid work that serves their sense of purpose. But this alignment is not always possible or necessary for a meaningful contribution.

9 What matters most is not that your job perfectly matches your calling, but that you find ways to live out your calling through whatever work circumstances allow.

5 Your calling often comes not from what you think you want to do but from what you notice needs doing—problems that trouble you, needs that move you to action, opportunities for service that capture your attention.

2 It grows from the intersection of your abilities and the world's needs, your passions and real problems that require solutions.

3 Sometimes calling reveals itself through what disturbs you—injustices that make you angry, suffering that breaks your heart, waste that offends your sense of stewardship.

4 Sometimes it appears through what delights you—beauty that inspires you to create more beauty, learning that compels you to share knowledge, healing that motivates you to serve others' recovery.

5 The person who pays attention to both their inner responses and outer circumstances often discovers their calling hiding in plain sight—in the conversations that energize them,

the problems they naturally notice, the activities that make them lose track of time.

6 Calling is not always dramatic or exotic. It may be as simple as bringing kindness to a harsh workplace, excellence to routine tasks, or mentorship to younger colleagues.

7 It may involve using your platform, however small, to advocate for causes you believe in, or leveraging your skills to support organizations whose mission moves you.

8 The key is recognizing that your particular combination of gifts, experiences, and circumstances creates unique opportunities for contribution that no one else can fulfill in exactly the same way.

9 Your calling is not necessarily your full-time job but it is your real work—the difference you are positioned to make during your temporary residence here.

6 When mortality clarifies your perspective on work, certain questions become urgent while others fade in importance.

2 "Will this matter in ten years?" becomes a filter for deciding where to invest your limited energy. "Does this serve something worthy of my brief time?" helps distinguish between busy work and meaningful work.

3 The knowledge that your career will end—whether through retirement, illness, or death—can liberate you from anxieties about professional advancement that consume those who imagine they have unlimited time.

4 It can also motivate greater urgency about using your current opportunities well, recognizing that chances to contribute may be more limited than you once assumed.

5 The person who grasps their temporal limits often becomes more selective about projects and commitments, saying yes only to work that aligns with their deeper values and sense of purpose.

6 They waste less time on office politics, status games, and

professional jealousies, focusing instead on doing their best work and helping others do theirs.

7 They become more generous with their knowledge and skills, understanding that hoarding expertise serves no good purpose if it dies with them.

8 They think more carefully about the legacy they are creating through their work—not just what they accomplish but how they accomplish it, not just what they build but how they treat people in the building process.

9 Mortality teaches that the character you display through your work matters as much as the results you achieve, that how you work is part of what you contribute to the world.

7

The sojourner's approach to work includes both appropriate ambition and healthy detachment—caring deeply about doing well while holding lightly to specific outcomes.

2 This is not the detachment of indifference but the detachment of wisdom—understanding that you can control your effort but not all variables that affect results.

3 You can pursue excellence without perfectionism, knowing that perfect work is less important than faithful work, that doing your best is sufficient even when your best produces imperfect results.

4 This perspective enables sustained effort without burnout, passionate engagement without obsession, professional pride without identity confusion.

5 When facing setbacks, failures, or career changes, the person who understands work as temporary stewardship adapts more readily than one whose identity depends entirely on professional success.

6 They can grieve the loss of work they loved without losing their sense of self, can move to new roles without feeling they have betrayed their previous commitments.

7 They understand that just as their work is temporary, so

are the specific forms it takes—what matters is maintaining the spirit of service through whatever changes circumstances require.

8 This flexibility becomes especially important as technology, economy, and society change the landscape of available work, making some roles obsolete while creating others that didn't previously exist.

9 The wise worker adapts to these changes not by abandoning their calling but by finding new ways to live it out in new circumstances.

8 Your attitude toward work affects not only your own experience but the experience of everyone whose work intersects with yours.

2 When you bring integrity to your labor, you make it easier for others to maintain their own integrity. When you approach tasks with excellence, you inspire similar commitment in colleagues.

3 When you treat work as stewardship rather than ownership, you collaborate more effectively, share credit more readily, and build up rather than tear down.

4 The leader who understands their role as temporary stewardship develops others rather than just using them, invests in systems that will outlast their tenure, and makes decisions based on long-term benefit rather than short-term personal advantage.

5 The employee who grasps the temporary nature of all work positions gives their best effort regardless of whether their compensation or recognition is perfect or meets their desired expecations, understanding that their character matters more than others' appreciation.

6 The colleague who sees work as contribution rather than competition supports others' success as well as their own, recognizing that everyone's growth serves the larger purpose

better than individual advancement at others' expense.

7 In this way, your understanding of work as temporary stewardship becomes a gift not only to yourself but to everyone whose journey intersects with yours in the workplace.

8 You help create work environments that serve human growth rather than just productivity, that respect people's dignity rather than just their usefulness.

9 As your time of active work draws toward its end—whether through planned retirement or unexpected circumstances—the stewardship model of labor provides a framework for transitioning gracefully.

2 You need not cling desperately to roles that once defined you, nor retreat into irrelevance believing your contributions are finished.

3 Instead, you can move naturally from direct responsibility to supportive presence, from leadership to mentorship, from doing the work to teaching others to do it well.

4 The knowledge and wisdom accumulated through years of faithful stewardship becomes your gift to those who will carry the work forward.

5 You can take satisfaction in what you contributed during your time of service without demanding that your particular methods or perspectives be preserved unchanged by your successors.

6 You can step aside gracefully, trusting that the work is larger than any individual worker, that new hands will find new ways to serve the same essential purposes.

7 This transition becomes easier when you have maintained interests and relationships beyond your professional role, when your identity includes but is not limited by your work.

8 The person who has understood work as stewardship rather than ownership finds it natural to pass along responsibility when the time comes, just as they once received it from others who preceded them.

9 They can look back with gratitude for the opportunity to have contributed, forward with hope for what others will accomplish, and inward with peace about having used their gifts well during their time of service.

10

Whether your work is prestigious or humble, well-compensated or poorly paid, publicly recognized or privately performed, the ultimate question is not how much you achieved but how faithfully you stewarded what was entrusted to you.

2 Did you use your abilities to serve purposes worthy of your brief time here? Did you approach your tasks with integrity and care? Did you contribute to the growth of others through your labor?

3 Did you treat your work as temporary responsibility rather than permanent possession, holding it with appropriate seriousness but not ultimate attachment?

4 The person who can answer these questions affirmatively has worked well, regardless of external measures of success or failure.

5 They have understood that work is not the purpose of life but one means of living purposefully, not the source of meaning but one expression of meaning.

6 They have grasped that their true legacy lies not in the specific projects they completed but in the spirit with which they approached all their projects, not in the positions they held but in how they held those positions.

7 For in the end, the work will continue without you, but the way you worked becomes part of who you are and who you encourage others to become.

8 Let your work, whatever its form, be an expression of your values rather than a contradiction of them, a service to something larger than yourself rather than merely a means of self-advancement.

9 Work as one who knows that time is limited, that opportunities to contribute are precious, that the chance to be useful in this world is a gift not to be wasted.

10 Work as a sojourner—passing through, not staying permanently, but leaving the work better for your faithful stewardship during the time it was placed in your care.

11 For this is the way of wisdom: to understand that while you cannot take your work with you when you go, you can take with you the character that your work helped to form, and you can leave behind the difference that your work made in the lives of others.

12 In this understanding, all honest work becomes sacred, all faithful labor becomes worship, and all good stewardship becomes a form of love offered to the world during your brief but meaningful journey through it.

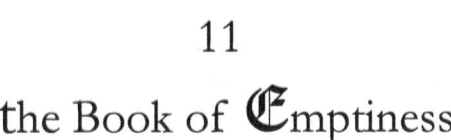

11

the Book of Emptiness

1 Consider this fundamental truth about the human condition: that which is empty seeks to be filled, as surely as water flows downhill and plants grow toward light.

2 Within each sojourner on this journey exist spaces that yearn for completion—the soul that hungers for meaning, the heart that thirsts for connection, the mind that craves understanding, the spirit that seeks purpose.

3 These empty places are not flaws in our design but essential features of our humanity, creating the capacity for growth, learning, and transformation.

4 Yet in these very spaces of emptiness lies both our greatest vulnerability and our greatest opportunity.

5 For the empty soul will be filled with something. The

vacant heart will attach to someone or something. The restless mind will occupy itself with thoughts and ideas. The question is not whether these spaces will be filled, but with what they will be filled.

6 The unaware sojourner stumbles through life allowing these empty spaces to be filled by whatever happens to be available—like a person dying of thirst who drinks from any puddle, not caring whether the water is pure or poisoned.

7 But the wise sojourner understands this fundamental law of human nature and takes responsibility for choosing what enters these sacred spaces within.

8 They recognize that emptiness is not the enemy to be feared but the fertile ground in which the seeds of their future self will be planted.

2 The soul's emptiness manifests as a deep longing for meaning, for purpose that transcends the daily routine of survival and comfort.

2 This sacred hunger drives humanity's greatest achievements—the creation of art that outlasts its creators, the pursuit of knowledge that benefits future generations, the sacrifice for causes larger than individual interest.

3 Yet when this emptiness goes unrecognized or unaddressed, it becomes vulnerable to false fillers that promise meaning but deliver only temporary distraction.

4 Some try to fill the soul's emptiness with material accumulation, believing that enough possessions will finally satisfy the deep longing within.

5 They collect experiences like trophies, relationships like achievements, accomplishments like medals, always searching for the next acquisition that will complete them.

6 Others attempt to fill their soul's void with ideology or fanaticism, surrendering their capacity for independent

thought to movements that promise absolute certainty in exchange for absolute loyalty.

7 Still others try to fill the emptiness with busyness itself, scheduling every moment so that silence never has a chance to reveal the hollow places within.

8 But the soul's true hunger is for connection with something eternal, something that gives weight and significance to the brief span of mortal existence.

9 It seeks not distraction from the questions of existence but engagement with them, not escape from the mystery of being human but immersion in its depths.

10 The aware sojourner recognizes this hunger and seeks to fill it with what truly nourishes: acts of service that connect them to purposes beyond themselves, pursuit of truth that expands understanding, creation of beauty that adds light to the world.

3 The heart's emptiness appears as loneliness, as the ache for connection that goes deeper than mere companionship.

2 The human heart was designed for relationship, for the giving and receiving of love, for the security that comes from being known and accepted by others.

3 When this need goes unmet, the heart becomes like parched earth, ready to absorb whatever moisture it encounters, regardless of whether that moisture nourishes or poisons.

4 Some fill their heart's emptiness with relationships that demand little but give less—connections based on mutual entertainment rather than mutual growth, associations that occupy time without enriching life.

5 Others attempt to satisfy their heart's hunger through relationships that consume rather than nourish, choosing partners who need them desperately rather than love them deeply.

6 The empty heart may seek filling through romantic obsession, believing that finding the perfect person will solve the problem of inner loneliness.

7 Or it may pursue social media connections that provide the illusion of relationship without the substance of true intimacy.

8 Some fill their heart's void with pets, hobbies, or causes, substituting these for the human connections they fear to pursue.

9 But the heart's deepest need is for authentic relationship—connections where masks can be removed, where vulnerability is met with acceptance, where individual growth is supported rather than threatened.

10 The wise sojourner seeks to fill their heart's emptiness with relationships that call forth their best self while accepting their current limitations.

11 They choose friends who challenge them to grow, partners who see their potential while loving their present reality, communities that support their authentic journey rather than demanding conformity.

12 They learn that the heart's emptiness is not filled by finding perfect people but by becoming someone capable of genuine love—first of themselves, then of others in all their imperfect humanity.

4 The mind's emptiness shows itself as boredom, restlessness, and the constant search for stimulation to occupy thoughts that otherwise turn inward toward uncomfortable questions.

2 The human mind was created for wonder, for the joy of discovery, for the satisfaction of understanding complex truths and beautiful ideas.

3 When deprived of meaningful mental nourishment, the mind becomes like a child left alone with nothing constructive

to do—it will find something to occupy itself, but that something may be destructive rather than beneficial.

4 Some fill their mind's emptiness with endless entertainment, moving from one diversion to another without pause for reflection or integration.

5 They consume shows, games, videos, and social media feeds like mental junk food, providing temporary satisfaction but no lasting nourishment.

6 Others fill the mental void with worry, rehearsing potential problems over and over, creating elaborate scenarios of future disaster to give their thoughts something to work on.

7 Still others occupy their minds with gossip, criticism, and judgment of others, using other people's lives as raw material for mental activity that produces nothing constructive.

8 Some attempt to fill their mental emptiness with conspiracy theories or extreme ideologies that provide simple explanations for complex realities, trading intellectual humility for the comfort of apparent certainty.

9 But the mind's true hunger is for growth, for learning that expands perspective and increases capacity for wisdom.

10 The aware sojourner feeds their mind with books that challenge assumptions, conversations with people who think differently, experiences that broaden understanding.

11 They seek education not just for practical advancement but for the joy of discovery, pursuing knowledge that may have no immediate application but enriches their capacity for thought.

12 They practice disciplines that strengthen mental capacity—meditation that trains attention, writing that clarifies thinking, discussion that sharpens reasoning.

13 They fill their mind's emptiness with questions worth pondering rather than answers that stop inquiry, with mysteries that invite exploration rather than certainties that end investigation.

5 The emotional emptiness within manifests as numbness, as the absence of feeling that creates its own kind of suffering.

2 Emotions are the colors of human experience, giving texture and meaning to events that would otherwise be merely factual occurrences.

3 When emotional capacity becomes deadened through trauma, disappointment, or simple neglect, the resulting emptiness creates a gray existence where nothing seems to matter deeply.

4 Some attempt to fill this emotional void with artificial stimulation—extreme sports, risky behaviors, or intense experiences that force feeling through overwhelming sensation.

5 Others try to jumpstart their emotional life through drama, creating or seeking conflict, crisis, or chaos because any feeling seems better than no feeling.

6 Some fill their emotional emptiness with substances that chemically induce feelings, trading authentic emotion for manufactured mood changes that leave them more depleted than before.

7 Others become addicted to emotional extremes, seeking relationships or situations that swing between ecstasy and despair because the intensity makes them feel alive.

8 But healthy emotion cannot be forced or manufactured—it emerges naturally from authentic engagement with life, from allowing yourself to be affected by beauty, moved by love, stirred by injustice.

9 The wise sojourner understands that emotional emptiness often results from protection mechanisms that once served a purpose but now prevent growth.

10 They work gently to reclaim their capacity for feeling, starting with small safe experiences of emotion and gradually expanding their tolerance for the full range of human feeling.

11 They fill their emotional emptiness not with artificial stimulation but with authentic experiences—genuine relationships, meaningful work, encounters with beauty, acts of service.

12 They learn that the goal is not constant happiness but emotional aliveness, the ability to feel appropriate responses to life's varied experiences.

6 The spiritual emptiness that many experience shows itself as a sense of disconnection from anything larger than personal concerns, a feeling of being adrift in a universe without meaning or purpose.

2 This emptiness may follow the loss of childhood faith, the disappointment with religious institutions, or simply the gradual realization that inherited beliefs no longer provide satisfactory answers to life's questions.

3 Some attempt to fill this spiritual void with substitutes that provide structure and community without requiring genuine faith—political movements, lifestyle philosophies, or wellness practices that promise transcendence through technique.

4 Others try to fill the emptiness with a return to childhood religion, hoping to recapture earlier certainty without acknowledging how their questions and understanding have evolved.

5 Still others attempt to fill their spiritual emptiness with materialism, convincing themselves that the physical world is all there is and that seeking anything beyond it is foolish.

6 Some pursue spiritual experiences through drugs, meditation retreats, or exotic practices, hoping for dramatic revelations that will instantly solve their sense of disconnection.

7 But authentic spiritual filling rarely comes through dramatic experiences or instant solutions—it grows through

patient cultivation of practices that connect the individual to something larger than themselves.

8 The wise sojourner approaches their spiritual emptiness with both honesty about their questions and openness to mystery that may not provide simple answers.

9 They fill this space not with borrowed certainties but with personal exploration, not with dogma but with experience, not with answers that end inquiry but with practices that deepen connection.

10 They may find spiritual nourishment in nature, in service to others, in the pursuit of justice, in the creation of beauty, in contemplative practices that quiet the mind and open the heart.

11 They understand that spiritual emptiness is not a problem to be solved but a space to be inhabited with reverence, a capacity for transcendence that makes humans more than mere biological machines.

7 The danger of unrecognized emptiness lies in its indiscriminate nature—empty spaces will be filled with whatever is available, regardless of whether that filling serves growth or stunts it.

2 Like a garden plot that will sprout weeds if not intentionally planted with desired crops, the empty places within us will be occupied by whatever influences we encounter most frequently.

3 In a culture that profits from human emptiness, countless forces compete to fill these spaces with products, ideas, and experiences that serve their interests rather than yours.

4 Advertisers study human emptiness like farmers study soil, learning exactly what promises will take root in which kinds of void.

5 They offer products to fill the soul's emptiness,

relationships to fill the heart's loneliness, entertainment to fill the mind's boredom, experiences to fill the spirit's disconnection.

6 Social media platforms design their interfaces to exploit emotional emptiness, providing just enough connection to keep users engaged but never enough to truly satisfy.

7 Political movements target spiritual emptiness, offering simple explanations and clear enemies to those hungry for meaning and purpose.

8 Consumer culture feeds on every form of emptiness, promising that the right purchase will finally complete whatever feels lacking within.

9 Without awareness of this dynamic, the sojourner becomes a passive consumer of whatever fills happen to be most aggressively marketed or easily available.

10 They mistake the temporary relief that comes from any filling for genuine nourishment, not recognizing that some substances that ease hunger in the short term create greater emptiness in the long term.

8 The path of wisdom begins with honest acknowledgment of where emptiness exists within you—which spaces ache to be filled, what hungers drive your choices, what voids make you vulnerable to poor filling.

2 This self-examination requires courage because it means looking directly at what feels lacking rather than staying distracted by constant activity.

3 It means asking difficult questions: What am I trying to fill with this relationship, this purchase, this habit, this pursuit?

4 Why do I feel restless when I'm alone with my thoughts? What makes me uncomfortable about silence, solitude, or stillness?

5 What emotions do I avoid feeling? What aspects of life do I stay too busy to contemplate?

6 This inventory of emptiness is not meant to create shame or despair but to create awareness that makes conscious choice possible.

7 Once you recognize where the empty spaces are, you can take responsibility for how they get filled rather than allowing the process to happen unconsciously.

8 The aware sojourner develops the discipline to pause before filling any emptiness, asking not just "Will this provide relief?" but "Will this provide nourishment?"

9 They learn to distinguish between quick fixes that provide temporary satisfaction and investments that create lasting fulfillment.

10 They understand that some emptiness is meant to remain empty for a time, serving as fertile space for future growth rather than being hastily filled with whatever is convenient.

11 Like a wise gardener who leaves some plots fallow to restore their nutrients, the conscious person sometimes chooses to sit with emptiness rather than rushing to fill it.

9 The art of conscious filling begins with identifying what truly nourishes each type of emptiness you experience.

2 For the soul's hunger for meaning, seek purposes that connect your individual life to something larger—causes that will matter beyond your lifetime, work that serves others, contributions that add light to the world.

3 Fill this space with books that expand your understanding of life's big questions, with conversations about matters of ultimate concern, with practices that connect you to whatever you understand as sacred.

4 For the heart's need for connection, choose relationships that call forth your authenticity rather than requiring you to perform or pretend.

5 Seek friendships based on mutual growth rather than

mutual entertainment, partnerships that support each person's becoming rather than demanding they remain static.

6 Fill this space with the practice of vulnerability, with the courage to let yourself be known, with the commitment to know others beyond their social masks.

7 For the mind's hunger for stimulation, provide challenges that stretch your thinking rather than content that merely occupies your attention.

8 Feed your mind with learning that expands your capacity for wisdom, with art that opens new ways of seeing, with questions that invite deeper exploration.

9 Fill this space with disciplines that strengthen mental capacity—reading that requires concentration, writing that clarifies thinking, discussion that sharpens reasoning.

10 For emotional emptiness, create safe opportunities to feel—through art that moves you, relationships that touch you, experiences that connect you to the full range of human emotion.

11 Fill this space with practices that restore emotional aliveness—time in nature, creative expression, physical activity that reconnects you with your body.

12 For spiritual emptiness, explore practices that connect you to mystery and transcendence—whether through traditional religion, personal spirituality, or secular practices that evoke wonder and reverence.

10

The conscious filling of emptiness requires patience because genuine nourishment takes time to integrate, unlike quick fixes that provide immediate but temporary relief.

2 Just as physical health improves gradually through consistent good nutrition rather than instant remedies, inner health develops through steady investment in what truly nourishes.

3 The person accustomed to fast-acting fillers must learn

to appreciate the slower but more lasting satisfaction that comes from authentic nourishment.

4 This means developing tolerance for the discomfort that comes between recognizing emptiness and finding healthy ways to address it.

5 It means learning to sit with longing rather than immediately reaching for whatever will make it stop, understanding that some hungers point toward growth opportunities that shouldn't be short-circuited.

6 The conscious sojourner learns to ask not just "What will make this emptiness go away?" but "What is this emptiness trying to tell me about what I need for growth?"

7 They understand that emptiness often signals readiness for the next stage of development, indicating that previous fillings have been outgrown and new ones are needed.

8 Like a hermit crab that must leave its shell when it outgrows it, human beings must sometimes experience emptiness as part of the natural process of growth into larger capacity.

9 The wise person learns to interpret certain forms of emptiness as invitations to expansion rather than problems to be solved quickly.

10 They develop the courage to remain empty longer if necessary to make room for filling that truly serves their evolution rather than merely their comfort.

11 One of the greatest challenges in conscious filling is learning to distinguish between what you think you need and what you actually need for growth and fulfillment.

2 Often the emptiness you feel in one area points to a need in a different area entirely—the person who feels socially empty may actually need more solitude to develop a stronger sense of self before seeking connection with others.

3 The individual who feels intellectually restless may need

emotional healing more than mental stimulation, since unprocessed feelings can block the mind's capacity for clear thinking.

4 Sometimes what feels like spiritual emptiness is actually the need for physical rest, or what seems like emotional numbness is the mind's need for new challenges.

5 The interconnected nature of human experience means that filling in one area often affects all others—addressing emotional needs may restore mental clarity, developing spiritual practices may improve relationships.

6 This is why conscious filling requires not just awareness of what feels empty but wisdom about what kind of nourishment will most effectively serve your overall growth.

7 It requires the humility to recognize that your immediate instincts about what you need may not always be accurate, especially if those instincts have been shaped by past patterns of unconscious filling.

8 The wise sojourner learns to experiment thoughtfully with different forms of nourishment, paying attention to which investments actually create lasting satisfaction and which provide only temporary relief.

9 They develop the patience to try approaches that may feel unfamiliar or initially uncomfortable, understanding that growth often requires moving beyond existing comfort zones.

10 They seek guidance from others who have successfully navigated similar emptiness, learning from the experience of those who have found authentic nourishment for the hungers they share.

12
As you become more skilled at conscious filling, you begin to recognize that emptiness and fullness are not permanent states but natural rhythms of human experience.

2 Just as breathing requires both emptying and filling the lungs, psychological health requires both periods of active filling and times of intentional emptying.

3 The person who tries to remain constantly full, never allowing any space for emptiness, becomes like a container with no room for anything new—stagnant rather than growing.

4 Conversely, the person who remains always empty, never allowing genuine filling, becomes like a vessel that serves no purpose—available but never useful.

5 The art of conscious living involves learning to move gracefully between these states, emptying what no longer serves to make room for what better serves your current growth.

6 This might mean letting go of relationships that have become more habit than nourishment, clearing mental space cluttered with old ideas that no longer fit your expanding understanding.

7 It might involve releasing emotional patterns that once protected you but now limit you, or spiritual beliefs that provided comfort in earlier stages but no longer support your evolving relationship with mystery.

8 The wise sojourner learns to see emptiness not as failure or loss but as capacity for new growth, space for better filling, opportunity for conscious choice about what enters their inner world.

9 They understand that the goal is not to eliminate emptiness but to relate to it consciously, filling it intentionally with what serves their highest development.

10 In this way, emptiness becomes not the enemy of fulfillment but its partner, creating the very space that makes meaningful filling possible.

11 The person who masters this art of conscious emptiness and filling discovers a form of inner freedom that those driven by unconscious hungers never know.

12 They find that by choosing consciously what fills their inner spaces, they become truly free—not from the human

need for nourishment, but free to seek nourishment that serves their deepest values and highest aspirations.

13 This is the way of the aware sojourner: to recognize emptiness as invitation, to approach filling as opportunity, and to understand that what fills the inner life ultimately determines the quality of the outer journey.

14 For in the end, you become what you consistently fill yourself with, shaped by the thoughts you think, the emotions you nurture, the relationships you invest in, the purposes you serve.

15 Choose wisely what enters the sacred spaces within you, for these choices more than any others determine who you become and what kind of journey you travel through this brief and precious life.

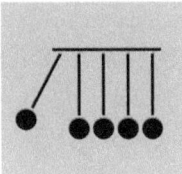

12

the Book of Predispositions

1 Consider, sojourner, the two streams that have shaped who you are: the nature you were born with and the nurture you received growing up. Like a riverbed and the water flowing through it, these forces together have shaped the path of your journey.

2 Your nature was set before you took your first breath. Your body type, your personality, your natural tendencies—these were woven into who you are from the beginning.

3 Some people are born naturally peaceful, others more restless. Some minds easily work with numbers, others better understand feelings. Some bodies are naturally strong, others need more care to work well.

4 These natural tendencies aren't good or bad in

themselves. They're simply the clay you were made from, each with different qualities that affect how you experience life.

5 Alongside nature flows nurture—the environments you grew up in, the words people spoke to you, the lessons you were taught, the hurts you experienced, and the healing you received.

6 Some people grow up surrounded by encouragement, others with neglect. Some receive helpful guidance and boundaries, others learn harmful lessons that twist their understanding. Some are protected from harm, others face storms that leave lasting damage.

7 Early experiences create pathways in your mind that remain long after childhood. What parents and teachers said still echoes years later. Early feelings of safety or danger still affect how you approach new situations today.

8 Both nature and nurture strongly influence you, but neither completely controls you. You aren't just your genes or just how you were raised. You're also a thinking being who can become aware and make choices.

9 So don't waste time arguing about which is more important—nature or nurture. Both have shaped you significantly, often in ways so mixed together they can't be separated.

10 Instead, focus on understanding these influences so you can navigate your life wisely rather than being unconsciously driven by forces you don't recognize or understand.

2 The sojourner who doesn't understand how they were formed walks like someone blindfolded, repeatedly stumbling over the same obstacles without understanding why the path seems so difficult.

2 Therefore, try to understand the nature you were born with. Watch your natural tendencies with curiosity instead of judgment. Notice what gives you energy and what drains you,

what comes easily and what's hard, what triggers strong reactions and what doesn't affect you much.

3 This isn't being self-centered—it's being wise. A carpenter must know how different woods work to use them skillfully. Similarly, you need to understand your particular qualities to navigate your journey effectively.

4 Ask yourself: Do you naturally enjoy being with people, or do you need alone time to recharge? Does your mind jump quickly between ideas or dive deeply into one subject? Does your body handle certain foods easily while struggling with others? Do you respond first with feelings or with thinking when challenged?

5 These patterns are like the grain in wood. Working with your natural grain rather than against it brings both effectiveness and peace. Constantly fighting against your nature creates needless struggle and leaves you with less strength for your journey.

6 Likewise, honestly examine how you were raised. What messages did you hear repeatedly growing up? What behaviors were rewarded or punished? What beliefs about yourself, others, and the world did you absorb before you were old enough to question them?

7 Some of this upbringing has equipped you well, giving you wisdom, resilience, and helpful ways of understanding. Be grateful for these gifts and for those who provided them, as they've strengthened your steps.

8 But some upbringing has burdened rather than helped you. False ideas about your worth, unhealthy expectations about relationships, misguided strategies for finding safety or love—these may have become deep patterns that now lead you away from a good life.

9 The sojourner who refuses to examine their upbringing walks carrying invisible baggage, wondering why the journey feels so hard yet unwilling to look at what weighs them down.

10 Self-awareness requires both courage and compassion. Courage to look honestly at how you've been shaped; compassion to recognize that both you and those who shaped you were doing the best you could with what you understood at the time.

11 Remember that awareness itself begins the change. The patterns of nature and nurture that remain hidden keep their full power over your journey. What is brought into the light can be worked with wisely.

3 After recognizing the forces that have formed you, unwise sojourners often make one of two mistakes: either completely giving in to these influences as unchangeable destiny or constantly fighting against them in exhausting rebellion.

2 The first mistake says, "This is just how I am, how I was made and raised. I can't help my reactions or change my path." This view denies the ability to grow and choose that is central to being human.

3 The second mistake says, "I reject everything about how I was made and raised. I'll create myself new through pure willpower." This proud view overestimates our ability to remake ourselves and underestimates how deeply our formation affects us.

4 The wise sojourner takes a different approach, neither passively accepting nor aggressively fighting against their formation, but working skillfully with it—like a sailor who neither ignores nor battles the wind but adjusts the sails to use its power.

5 See your natural strengths not as reasons for pride but as special tools given to you for your journey and for helping others.

6 A naturally compassionate heart, an analytical mind, a resilient body, a creative spirit—each is a gift to use well, not a personal achievement.

7 See your natural limitations not as flaws to hide but as invitations to connection and community.

8 No one has all strengths.

9 Your limitations create spaces where others' gifts become essential, weaving the connections that support all sojourners.

10 For the helpful aspects of your upbringing—the wisdom, values, and perspectives given by family, teachers, and community—receive these not as rigid rules but as foundations that can grow and develop as your understanding deepens.

11 And for the harmful aspects of your upbringing—the false beliefs, unhealthy patterns, and wounds received—approach these not with bitter rejection of everything connected to them, but with discernment that keeps what's true while releasing what's distorted.

12 The sojourner wastes precious energy fighting battles that don't need fighting. You don't need to wage war against being introverted or extroverted, emotionally sensitive or analytical, or against your physical build or brain wiring. Better to understand these aspects of yourself and work wisely with them.

13 Likewise, you don't need to either blindly accept or completely reject the worldview you were given.

14 Wisdom lies in thoughtfully evaluating what you received, keeping what's good, releasing what's harmful, and staying open to new understanding as your journey continues.

15 Remember that change comes not mainly through fighting against what is, but through developing new patterns alongside the old, gradually strengthening alternative pathways until they become more natural.

4 Within every sojourner exist two powerful forces that often seem to oppose each other: the drive toward self-preservation

and the pull toward self-destruction. These aren't moral categories of good and evil, but natural tensions within the human journey.

2 Alongside preservation exists its opposite force: the pull toward self-transcendence that sometimes appears as self-destruction. This shows up in the willingness to risk comfort for growth, to sacrifice immediate pleasure for deeper purpose, to release attachments, to question certainties, to venture into unknown territories, and to surrender the smaller self for something larger.

3 This transcending force also carries essential wisdom. It enables courage, generosity, and growth beyond comfortable limits. It makes possible giving up ego for love, trading security for purpose, and being willing to be transformed through difficult experiences. Without it, the journey would become merely survival without meaning or growth.

4 Yet this same transcending force, when operating without awareness, can become truly self-destructive: reckless risk-taking, ignoring legitimate needs, disrespecting the body, rejecting healthy boundaries, breaking necessary structures, and being drawn to experiences that damage rather than transform.

5 The sojourner often treats these forces as enemies to defeat rather than energies to navigate. Some try to eliminate all risk and uncertainty, creating rigid lives that preserve safety but lose vitality. Others glorify risk and intensity, creating chaotic lives that pursue transcendence but sacrifice sustainability.

6 The wise sojourner understands that both forces have appropriate times and uses. There are times when preservation should take priority—when the body needs rest, when resources must be gathered, when boundaries need strengthening, when stability is needed for healing or growth.

7 And there are times when the transcending impulse

should lead—when comfort must be risked for purpose, when possessions must be shared, when certainties must be questioned, when the familiar must be left for new territories that call to the heart.

8 This isn't a simple balance achieved once and maintained forever. It's an ongoing navigation that requires discernment in each new situation of the journey. The question isn't "Which force is right?" but "Which wisdom does this particular situation need?"

5 Many teachings suggest that sojourners should seek perfect balance between competing forces, as if the ideal life is like scales with equal weight on both sides. But the journey doesn't work through perfect balance maintained at all times.

2 Think instead about navigation. A skilled sailor doesn't try to balance the forces of wind and current equally at all times. Instead, they work with these forces appropriately based on their destination, the weather, and their boat's capabilities.

3 Sometimes the sail is fully open to catch the strongest winds; other times it's partly closed to prevent capsizing in a storm. Sometimes the current is used for speed; other times it must be crossed to avoid being carried off course. The skill is in discernment and appropriate response, not in keeping a single, unchanging position.

4 Similarly, the sojourner must navigate the forces of nature and nurture, of preservation and transcendence, with wisdom rather than rigid rules. No single approach works for all seasons, all situations, or all people.

5 In some seasons, you must honor your natural need for solitude and pull back from too much interaction. In others, you must stretch beyond comfort to connect even when it's difficult. Neither approach is always right or wrong; the wisdom is in knowing what each situation needs.

6 In some circumstances, you should draw strongly on the

preserving instinct—setting clear boundaries with those who cause harm, securing necessary resources during times of scarcity, or creating stability during periods of healing or transition.

7 In other circumstances, the transcending impulse should be given more expression—taking relational risks for deeper connection, releasing attachments that have become too important, questioning beliefs that have hardened into rigid dogma, or stepping into unknown territories when growth requires it.

8 The sojourner who insists on a single formula for all situations—whether complete security or constant risk, total self-sufficiency or complete dependence, rigid consistency or endless adaptation—will find their journey unnecessarily limited.

9 True wisdom comes not from finding the perfect middle point between extremes but in recognizing which energy, which approach, which aspect of your nature or nurture is most appropriate to use in each unique situation you face.

10 This navigation requires both deep self-knowledge and present awareness. You must understand your natural tendencies, the patterns established through your upbringing, and the particular ways preservation and transcendence show up in your life. And you must stay awake to the specific needs of each new situation rather than responding with habitual patterns regardless of context.

11 The sojourner who navigates wisely doesn't waste energy fighting against their natural personality or formative experiences. Nor do they surrender all choice to these influences.

12 Instead, they work skillfully with what has been given and what has been learned, drawing on different aspects as each new territory requires.

13 This way, what might seem like limitations become

specialized tools for the journey. The naturally cautious sojourner brings valuable perspective when risks need careful assessment. The naturally adventurous sojourner helps others move beyond comfortable stagnation. The emotional sensitivity formed through difficult experiences becomes capacity for compassion. The analytical distance developed as protection becomes clarity in complex situations.

14 Remember that no single approach works for everything. A skilled worker doesn't use a hammer for every task but selects the right tool for each specific job. Similarly, the wise sojourner draws on different aspects of their nature and nurture according to what each situation truly needs.

15 The journey isn't about achieving perfect balance but about navigating with awareness, discernment, and courage, using all that you are and all that has shaped you to serve your authentic path and the greater good of all fellow sojourners.

13

the Book of Voices

1 Within each sojourner on this journey lives two voices, speaking constantly about the choices that shape the path ahead.

2 One voice shouts with the volume of immediate desire, urgent need, and pressing fear. It demands attention, drowns out other sounds, and insists on instant satisfaction.

3 This loud voice speaks the language of self-preservation: "Take what you can get. Protect yourself first. Others will do the same to you if you don't do it to them first."

4 It whispers seductively of shortcuts and compromises: "No one will know. Everyone else does it. You deserve this. The rules don't apply to you."

5 This voice grows louder in times of stress, fear, or want,

filling the mind with justifications for choices that serve the self at the expense of others.

6 But there is another voice within—quieter, gentler, easily overlooked amid the noise of daily life.

7 This quiet voice speaks not from desire but from wisdom, not from fear but from love, not from scarcity but from abundance.

8 It carries within it the accumulated goodness of countless generations who have walked before you—the conscience of humanity itself, refined through ages of learning what builds up and what tears down.

9 Listen carefully, and you will recognize its familiar whispers: "This is not who you want to be. There is a better way. You know what is right."

2 The quiet voice within you is not your own creation but your inheritance—a gift passed down through the long line of human experience.

2 It carries the wisdom of parents who taught you to share, of teachers who showed you fairness, of neighbors who demonstrated kindness to strangers.

3 It holds the truth of philosophers who reasoned toward justice, of prophets who called for mercy, of ordinary people who chose courage over comfort in moments that mattered.

4 This voice speaks from the collective learning of humanity about what creates growth communities and what destroys them, what builds lasting happiness and what leads to emptiness.

5 It knows that generosity creates abundance while hoarding creates scarcity, that truth builds trust while deception destroys it, that compassion heals while cruelty wounds.

6 The quiet voice remembers lessons learned through centuries of human trial and error—that power without

restraint corrupts, that might without right fails, that winning without honor is losing.

7 When you listen to this voice, you connect not only with your better self but with the better angels of human nature itself.

8 You join the company of all those throughout history who chose the harder path because it was the right path, who sacrificed immediate gain for lasting good.

3 In youth, the loud voice often drowns out the quiet one. Young minds, full of energy and empty of experience, frequently choose the path of immediate gratification over long-term wisdom.

2 This is neither surprising nor shameful—it is the natural condition of those who have not yet learned the cost of poor choices or discovered the rewards of patient virtue.

3 The young person hears the quiet voice but dismisses it as the overcaution of those who have forgotten what it means to truly live.

4 They mistake recklessness for courage, selfishness for strength, and rebellion for independence.

5 "I know better," they think. "The old ways don't apply to me. I can handle the consequences."

6 And so they make decisions that seem wise in the moment but reveal their foolishness over time—choices that bring temporary pleasure but lasting regret, immediate gain but eventual loss.

7 Yet this season of poor listening serves a purpose in the larger journey of wisdom.

8 For it is often only through experiencing the bitter fruit of ignoring the quiet voice that we learn to value its guidance.

9 The burned child learns to respect fire. The person who has suffered the consequences of selfish choices learns to appreciate the wisdom of considering others.

4 Fortunately, life offers second chances to those willing to learn from their mistakes.

2 The decisions made in youth, though they may create difficulties, rarely determine the entire course of a life. Time provides opportunity for correction, for growth, for redemption.

3 The relationship that ended badly can teach you how to love better. The career choice that proved wrong can lead you toward work more suited to your gifts.

4 The financial mistakes that created hardship can develop wisdom about money that serves you well in later years.

5 The trust that was betrayed can make you more discerning without making you cynical.

6 Each mistake carries within it the seeds of future wisdom, if you are willing to learn rather than simply regret.

7 As you mature, you begin to recognize the pattern: the times when you listened to the quiet voice led to outcomes you can be proud of, while the times you ignored it led to consequences you wish you could change.

8 This recognition gradually shifts the balance of attention from the loud voice to the quiet one.

9 You begin to pause before important decisions, creating space for the quiet voice to be heard above the clamor of immediate desire.

10 You develop the discipline to ask not just "What do I want?" but "What is right? What will I be proud of later? What serves not just me but all who are affected by my choice?"

5 The paradox of the quiet voice is this: though it speaks more softly than the voice of selfishness, following its guidance brings greater power and confidence.

2 When you act in harmony with the quiet voice, you act in alignment with the deeper currents of life itself.

3 You discover that honesty, though sometimes difficult in the moment, creates a foundation of trust that supports all your relationships.

4 You find that generosity, though it requires sacrifice, creates abundance that mere accumulation cannot match.

5 You learn that humility, though it feels like weakness, generates respect that arrogance destroys.

6 The person who consistently follows the quiet voice develops an inner confidence that does not depend on external validation or circumstances.

7 They know they are living according to principles that have stood the test of time, making choices that align with their deepest values.

8 This creates a stability that those who live by the loud voice never know—the peace that comes from integrity, the strength that comes from moral clarity.

9 Even when such choices lead to temporary disadvantage or loss, the person who follows the quiet voice retains their self-respect and sleeps well at night.

10 They may lose money, position, or popularity, but they keep their soul intact.

6 Learning to hear the quiet voice requires cultivating the art of stillness in a world designed to keep you constantly moving.

2 The loud voice thrives in noise, hurry, and distraction. It feeds on anxiety, urgency, and the pressure of immediate decision-making.

3 The quiet voice emerges in silence, solitude, and reflection. It speaks most clearly when the mind is calm and the heart is open.

4 Therefore, create regular spaces of quiet in your life—moments when you step away from the demands and distractions that drown out subtle wisdom.

5 This might be early morning contemplation before the day's demands begin, evening walks that provide space for reflection, or simply pausing before important decisions to ask what your deepest wisdom suggests.

6 In these quiet moments, pay attention to the subtle promptings that arise—the gentle nudge toward kindness, the soft warning against a choice that feels wrong, the quiet suggestion of a better way.

7 Notice the difference between the voice that says "I want" and the voice that says "This is good."

8 Learn to distinguish between the anxiety-driven thoughts that circle endlessly and the calm knowing that points toward right action.

9 The more you practice this listening, the clearer the quiet voice becomes, until you can hear it even amid the noise of daily life.

7

The quiet voice often speaks contrary to the values celebrated in your culture, challenging you to swim against currents of popular opinion.

2 When your society worships wealth, the quiet voice reminds you that contentment is true prosperity.

3 When your community celebrates fame, the quiet voice whispers that character matters more than reputation.

4 When your peers pursue pleasure above all else, the quiet voice suggests that meaning brings deeper satisfaction than entertainment.

5 When those around you justify cutting corners, the quiet voice insists that integrity is worth the extra effort.

6 This creates tension between fitting in and being true to your deeper wisdom, between social acceptance and moral clarity.

7 The person who consistently chooses to follow the quiet voice may find themselves sometimes lonely, misunderstood, or criticized by those who have chosen differently.

8 Yet they also discover the companionship of others who have made similar choices—a fellowship of those who value substance over appearance, depth over surface, truth over convenience.

9 They find that living by the quiet voice attracts others who are also seeking to live with integrity, creating relationships based on shared values rather than mutual exploitation.

10 Most importantly, they maintain their connection to their own authentic self, avoiding the spiritual emptiness that comes from constantly betraying one's own deepest knowledge of what is best and what is not best.

8 As you grow in your ability to hear and follow the quiet voice, you begin to understand that it speaks not only about individual choices but about your role in the larger human community.

2 The quiet voice reminds you that your actions ripple outward, affecting not only your own life but the lives of those around you and even those who will come after you.

3 It calls you to consider not just immediate consequences but long-term effects, not just personal benefit but collective good.

4 When facing a decision about how to treat an employee, the quiet voice asks not just what is legal but what is just.

5 When considering how to respond to someone who has wronged you, it suggests not just what feels satisfying but what might lead to healing.

6 When choosing how to spend your resources, it prompts you to consider not just your own needs but the needs of those who have less.

7 The quiet voice recognizes that individual growth and community growth are interconnected, that what harms others ultimately harms the self, and what serves the common good serves individual well-being as well.

8 It calls you to be a contributor to the sum of goodness in the world rather than merely a consumer of its resources.

9 This larger perspective transforms even mundane decisions into opportunities for moral choice, chances to add light rather than darkness to the human experience.

9 The quiet voice speaks most clearly about the legacy you are creating through your daily choices—the story you are writing with your life.

2 It asks persistently: "What kind of person are you becoming through these choices? What kind of world are you helping to create? What will be the final accounting of your time here?"

3 The loud voice focuses on the present moment—what you can get now, what you can avoid now, what will make you feel better now.

4 The quiet voice takes the longer view, considering what your choices today will create for tomorrow, what patterns you are establishing, what habits you are forming.

5 It reminds you that every choice is both an individual decision and a vote for the kind of world you want to live in.

6 When you choose honesty, you vote for a world where truth can be trusted. When you choose kindness, you vote for a world where compassion prevails.

7 When you choose courage in the face of injustice, you vote for a world where the weak are protected. When you choose generosity despite your own limitations, you vote for a world where abundance is shared.

8 The quiet voice understands that these individual votes matter, that they accumulate over time, that they influence others through example and inspiration.

9 It calls you to consider what kind of ancestor you want to be—not just to your biological descendants but to all who will inherit the world you are helping to shape.

10 There will be times when following the quiet voice requires significant sacrifice, when doing right comes at considerable cost.

2 In these moments, the loud voice will shout its protests: "This is foolish! You're throwing away your advantage! No one else would do this!"

3 The quiet voice responds more gently but with unshakeable conviction: "This is who you are meant to be. This is what it means to be human at your best. This is how you become worthy of your own respect."

4 These are the defining moments of a life—when the choice between self-interest and higher purpose becomes unavoidable, when character is revealed through action.

5 The person who has practiced listening to the quiet voice in smaller matters finds the strength to follow it in larger ones.

6 They discover that the confidence built through years of moral consistency provides courage for moments that demand exceptional integrity.

7 They learn that the peace that comes from living according to their deepest values is worth more than any external reward they might have gained by compromising those values.

8 Such choices often go unnoticed by the world, unrecorded in history books, uncelebrated in public forums.

9 But they are noticed by the quiet voice itself, which grows stronger and clearer with each decision to honor its guidance.

10 They are witnessed by your own soul, which gains dignity and power through each choice to do right regardless of personal cost.

11 The journey of learning to listen to the quiet voice is the journey of becoming fully human.

2 It is the path from being driven by instinct and impulse to being guided by wisdom and love.

3 It is the transformation from living reactively to living purposefully, from being tossed about by circumstances to being anchored in principles.

4 This journey takes a lifetime, and perhaps that is as it should be. The art of hearing and following the quiet voice deepens with experience, grows stronger through practice, becomes clearer through the wisdom that comes only through time.

5 The mistakes of youth teach appreciation for the guidance of conscience. The consequences of poor choices develop hunger for better wisdom.

6 The satisfaction that comes from right choices, even difficult ones, builds commitment to continue listening when the next decision arises.

7 Gradually, the quiet voice becomes not just an occasional visitor but a trusted friend, not just a voice you hear but a part of who you are.

8 You begin to recognize it as your truest self speaking—the part of you that is connected to all that is good in human nature, all that is wise in human experience, all that is noble in human possibility.

9 To follow this voice is to join the great company of those throughout history who have chosen the harder path because it was the better path, who have sacrificed immediate gain for lasting good.

12 In the end, the power of the quiet voice lies not in its volume but in its truth, not in its insistence but in its wisdom, not in its promises but in its reliability.

2 It never lies to you, never leads you astray, never asks you to do anything that will diminish your humanity or harm your soul.

3 It may ask you to do difficult things, costly things, unpopular things—but never wrong things.

4 The person who learns to trust this voice discovers a form of guidance more reliable than any external authority, more trustworthy than any human counselor, more enduring than any temporary advantage.

5 They find within themselves access to the accumulated wisdom of the human race, the moral insight of countless generations who have struggled with the same choices between selfishness and service, between fear and love, between what is easy and what is right.

6 This is your inheritance as a human being—not just the capacity for reason and emotion, but the capacity for moral wisdom, for ethical insight, for choices that serve not just survival but meaning.

7 The quiet voice is how this inheritance speaks to you, how the best of human nature makes itself known in your individual life.

8 Listen for it. Trust it. Follow it. In doing so, you honor not only your own highest potential but the highest potential of humanity itself.

9 For in the end, the quiet voice within you is not separate from the quiet voice within others—it is the same voice, speaking the same truths, calling all people toward the same light.

10 When you listen to it, you join the chorus of all who have chosen wisdom over foolishness, love over fear, service over selfishness.

11 This is the voice that builds civilizations, that heals wounds, that creates beauty, that serves justice, that offers hope.

12 This is the voice that makes us human at our best, and it is always speaking, always available, always ready to guide you toward your highest good and the good of all.

13 In chambers dark where shadows creep, And conscience stirs from restless sleep,

2 Between the worlds of joy and woe, The whispers come, then whispers go—

3 Listen to the quiet voice in the house.

4 The pendulum of thought swings wide, As sickness, health, walk side by side.

5 What mortal frame can hope to last When time's swift current flows so fast?

6 Listen to the quiet voice in the house.

7 Through corridors of doubt I roam, Seeking truth within this home,

8 Yet meaning hides behind the veil, While emptiness leaves spirits pale—

9 Listen to the quiet voice in the house.

10 When death's cold fingers brush the door, And life clings desperate to the floor,

11 The battle rages, silent, deep, In rooms where ancient secrets keep—

12 Listen to the quiet voice in the house.

13 What ghostly forms in corners dwell, With tales of heaven, hints of hell?

14 The soul's dark attic, cluttered, vast, Holds future promise, haunted past—

15 Listen to the quiet voice in the house.

16 Between the tolling of the bell, Between the heaven and the hell,

17 Between the laughter and the tears, Between the courage and the fears—

18 Listen to the quiet voice in the house.

19 The war within shall never cease, Yet wisdom offers fleeting peace.

20 For those who pause amid the strife To hear the gentle truths of life—

21 Listen to the quiet voice in the house.

22 In chambers of the heart's deep keep, Where neither mind nor eyes can peep,

23 The still, small voice that knows the way Will guide the soul through night to day—

24 Listen to the quiet voice in the house.

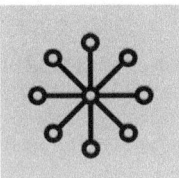

14

the Book of Choices

1 Each day of your journey as a sojourner presents you with countless choices, from the moment you open your eyes until you close them again in sleep.

2 What to eat, what to wear, what to say, where to go, how to spend your time, who to spend it with—these decisions shape not only your day but the direction of your entire journey.

3 Yet most people make these choices as if they had unlimited time, endless opportunities, and infinite chances to try again.

4 They delay important decisions while making trivial ones quickly, spending hours choosing what to watch but minutes deciding how to treat others.

5 But the sojourner who truly understands the temporary nature of this journey approaches choices differently.

6 When you know your time here is limited, every choice carries weight because every moment matters.

7 The decision to speak words of encouragement or remain silent could be the last chance to lift someone's spirit.

8 The choice to forgive or hold a grudge could determine whether a relationship ends in peace or pain.

9 The option to pursue meaningful work or settle for mere income could be the difference between a life of purpose and a life of regret.

10 Knowing you are a sojourner does not make choices easier, but it makes them clearer.

11 When you understand that this is not a rehearsal but the actual performance, you pay closer attention to your lines, your timing, and your role in the greater story.

2 The awareness of mortality brings both urgency and peace to the art of choosing.

2 Urgency, because you recognize that some opportunities will not come again, that some doors close permanently, that some moments for action pass and do not return.

3 Peace, because you also understand that you cannot do everything, be everything, or experience everything—and this limitation is not failure but simply the nature of finite existence.

4 The person who tries to keep all options open ends up choosing nothing, paralyzed by the fear of closing any door.

5 But the sojourner knows that choosing one path necessarily means not choosing others, and this is not loss but focus.

6 When you accept that you cannot have everything, you become free to choose what matters most.

7 When you embrace the fact that every yes requires several nos, you gain the power to say yes with conviction.

8 The temporary nature of life does not make choices less important but more important—not because the consequences last forever, but because the time to experience those consequences is so brief and precious.

9 Better to choose imperfectly and live fully than to choose perfectly and live barely.

10 Better to risk making the wrong choice than to make no choice at all.

3 In a world of endless options, the abundance of choices can become a curse rather than a blessing.

2 The grocery store offers fifty types of cereal, the streaming service presents thousands of shows, the online store shows hundreds of products to purchase.

3 This multiplication of options creates what wise people call the paralysis of choice—the more alternatives available, the harder it becomes to choose any of them.

4 Each option represents a path not taken, a possibility sacrificed, a door closed forever.

5 The fear of missing out on something better keeps many people from committing to anything good.

6 But the sojourner who understands the brevity of life develops a different relationship with choice.

7 They recognize that the perfect choice is often the enemy of the good choice, that waiting for the ideal option often means missing the adequate one.

8 They understand that most choices are reversible, most paths lead somewhere interesting, and most mistakes are survivable.

9 The clarity that comes from knowing your time is limited cuts through the fog of endless deliberation.

10 When you know you will not be here forever, you cannot afford to spend forever deciding.

11 The sojourner learns to choose decisively, act boldly,

and adjust course when necessary rather than remaining frozen by the fear of choosing wrong.

4 Many people think that moral choices are always between good and evil, right and wrong.

2 But the deepest struggles of the conscious sojourner often involve choosing between good and better, between two worthy paths that lead in different directions.

3 Should you spend your evening reading to expand your mind or visiting with friends to nurture relationships?

4 Should you accept a job that pays well but requires long hours away from family, or one that pays less but allows more time for what matters most?

5 These choices between competing goods test the sojourner's wisdom more than obvious choices between right and wrong.

6 When the choice is between helping a neighbor and helping a stranger, between supporting your family and serving your community, between personal growth and service to others, easy answers disappear.

7 The sojourner must develop the ability to weigh values, to understand priorities, to recognize that choosing one good thing sometimes requires sacrificing another.

8 This does not make the choice wrong, but it does make it complex, requiring wisdom beyond simple rule-following.

9 In these moments, the temporary nature of life becomes a guide rather than a burden.

10 Ask yourself: When I look back from the end of my journey, which choice will I be glad I made? Which path will seem to have led toward what mattered most?

5 The sojourner who chooses wisely learns to distinguish between urgent and important, between what demands immediate attention and what deserves continued focus.

2 Urgent matters shout for attention—the ringing phone, the

approaching deadline, the crisis that needs immediate response.

3 Important matters speak more quietly—the relationship that needs nurturing, the skill that needs developing, the dream that needs pursuing.

4 Because urgent matters make more noise, they often crowd out important ones, leaving people busy but unfulfilled, reactive but not purposeful.

5 The awareness of mortality helps clarify this difference.

6 At the end of your sojourn, you will not regret the urgent emails you failed to answer immediately, but you may regret the important conversations you never had.

7 You will not wish you had attended more meetings, but you might wish you had spent more time with those you love.

8 You will not mourn the tasks left undone, but you may mourn the dreams left unpursued.

9 The sojourner learns to let some urgent things wait while tending to important things that cannot wait forever.

10 They understand that busy is not the same as productive, that full is not the same as meaningful, that urgent is not the same as significant.

11 When you know your time is limited, you become protective of how you spend it, choosing importance over urgency whenever possible.

6 Every choice creates consequences that ripple outward through time, affecting not only the chooser but others whose lives intersect with theirs.

2 The sojourner who understands this carries a sense of responsibility for their choices that goes beyond personal preference or immediate benefit.

3 The parent who chooses patience over irritation shapes their child's understanding of love.

4 The employee who chooses integrity over convenience influences their workplace culture.

5 The citizen who chooses engagement over apathy affects their community's future.

6 Because these consequences extend beyond the sojourner's brief stay, each choice becomes an act of stewardship for those who will remain after the choice-maker has departed.

7 This does not mean becoming paralyzed by the weight of consequence, but it does mean choosing with awareness of impact.

8 The sojourner asks not only "What do I want?" but "What will this choice create in the world? How will it affect others? What legacy will it leave?"

9 This broader perspective often clarifies difficult decisions, helping distinguish between choices that serve only the self and choices that serve the larger good.

10 Sometimes the choice that serves others also serves the self; sometimes it requires sacrifice.

11 But the sojourner who chooses with awareness of consequence lives with the satisfaction of knowing their brief presence made a positive difference.

7 One of the greatest challenges facing the conscious chooser is learning to live peacefully with the consequences of their decisions without falling into the trap of endless regret.

2 Every choice involves trade-offs, and every trade-off involves loss.

3 The path chosen prevents walking other paths; the yes spoken requires saying no to alternatives; the commitment made limits future options.

4 Those who cannot accept this reality of choosing live in constant regret, always wondering "what if," always second-guessing their decisions, always believing the grass is greener on paths not taken.

5 But regret is a prison that keeps you trapped in the past

instead of engaged with the present, focused on what might have been instead of what still might be.

6 The wise sojourner makes peace with the nature of choice itself—that it requires giving up some possibilities to pursue others, that it involves risk without guarantee of outcome.

7 They understand that making no choice is also a choice, that avoiding decision does not avoid consequence, that trying to keep all options open usually means fully pursuing none.

8 When facing the results of a choice that did not turn out as hoped, the sojourner asks not "How can I change the past?" but "How can I learn from this experience? What wisdom can I gain? How can I choose better next time?"

9 They recognize that even poor choices often lead to valuable learning, that detours sometimes reveal better destinations, that what seems like failure in the moment may prove to be redirection toward something better.

10 The sojourner focuses on the choices still to be made rather than endlessly relitigating choices already made.

8 The temporary nature of life does not make choices meaningless but gives them a poignant significance, like the last verses of a beautiful song or the final scenes of a moving story.

2 Because you cannot choose forever, each choice carries the weight of finite opportunity.

3 Because you will not be here always, how you choose to be here now matters deeply.

4 The sojourner develops the ability to choose with both courage and humility—courage to make decisions without perfect information, humility to accept that not every choice will prove wise.

5 They learn to choose authentically, based on their own values and understanding rather than on others' expectations or society's pressures.

6 They choose consistently, allowing their decisions to flow from stable principles rather than changing moods or circumstances.

7 They choose purposefully, asking how each decision serves their deepest values and highest aspirations.

8 They choose compassionately, considering the impact of their choices on others who share this brief journey.

9 The awareness of mortality does not paralyze the sojourner with the weight of choosing but frees them to choose boldly, knowing that time is precious and should not be wasted on indecision.

10 They understand that perfect choices are impossible but good choices are always available to those willing to think clearly and act decisively.

9 As the sojourner grows in wisdom, they begin to recognize patterns in their choosing that either serve their growth or hinder it.

2 They notice whether they tend to choose based on fear or hope, on immediate pleasure or long-term satisfaction, on others' approval or their own integrity.

3 They observe whether their choices consistently move them toward the person they want to become or away from that ideal.

4 This self-awareness allows for better choosing over time, as they learn from experience which kinds of decisions lead to fulfillment and which lead to emptiness.

5 The mature sojourner develops what might be called a "choosing philosophy"—a clear understanding of what values guide their decisions, what principles govern their selections, what hopes animate their preferences.

6 This philosophy serves as a compass when specific choices are difficult, providing direction when the path forward is unclear.

7 It helps distinguish between choices that align with their authentic self and choices that satisfy only social expectations or temporary desires.

8 The sojourner who chooses from a clear philosophy lives with greater integrity, as their actions flow from their values rather than from impulse or pressure.

9 They may still make mistakes, but they make them honestly, choosing badly rather than choosing hypocritically.

10 This authenticity in choosing creates a coherent life story, where decisions build upon each other toward meaningful purposes rather than contradicting each other in random directions.

10

The deepest choice that every sojourner must make is not about external circumstances but about internal attitude—how to respond to the conditions of temporary existence itself.

2 Will you choose gratitude or complaint about the time you have been given?

3 Will you choose engagement or withdrawal from the challenges of mortal life?

4 Will you choose hope or despair about the possibilities that remain even within limited time?

5 Will you choose love or fear as your primary response to the uncertainty of how much time you have?

6 These fundamental attitudes color every other choice, determining whether your sojourn becomes an adventure or an ordeal, a gift to be treasured or a burden to be endured.

7 The sojourner who chooses gratitude finds reasons for thanksgiving even in difficult circumstances, recognizing that existence itself is an unearned gift.

8 The one who chooses engagement discovers that meaningful activity makes time feel both precious and sufficient, that purpose transforms even routine choices into significant ones.

9 The sojourner who chooses hope maintains faith in possibility even when current conditions seem discouraging, believing that change remains possible until the final moment of the journey.

10 The one who chooses love as their fundamental stance finds that this choice influences every other decision, creating a coherent life oriented toward connection rather than protection, service rather than selfishness.

11 These deep choices about attitude and approach prove more significant than most specific choices about external circumstances, shaping the quality of the entire sojourn regardless of its particular events.

11

In the end, the sojourner learns that the art of choosing well is one of the most important skills to develop during the brief time allotted for growth and learning.

2 How you choose reveals who you are, shapes who you become, and influences what you contribute to the ongoing story of humanity.

3 The choices made by previous sojourners created the world you inherited; the choices you make will influence the world you leave behind.

4 This continuity of choice across generations gives weight and meaning to individual decisions, connecting your brief journey to the larger human story.

5 The sojourner who chooses wisely becomes a good ancestor, making decisions that serve not only their own journey but also the journeys of those who will follow.

6 They understand that their choices matter not because they last forever but because they contribute to patterns of human behavior that either build up or tear down the communities and cultures that outlast individual lives.

7 In this way, the temporary nature of the sojourner's stay makes their choices more rather than less significant, as each

decision becomes an opportunity to add light rather than darkness to the human experience.

8 Choose, then, with awareness of this significance. Choose with knowledge of your mortality and appreciation for your opportunity.

9 Choose decisively when decision is required, patiently when patience serves wisdom, courageously when courage is needed for integrity.

10 Choose with hope for the future, wisdom from the past, and presence in the current moment.

11 For in the end, you will be remembered not for how long you stayed but for how well you chose while you were here.

12 And you will rest peacefully when your choosing is done, knowing that you used the gift of free will to serve purposes larger than temporary comfort, values deeper than immediate pleasure, and goals more lasting than personal advantage.

13 This is the way of the wise sojourner: to choose as one who knows that choices matter, that time is limited, and that how you choose determines not just what you experience but who you become during your brief and precious passage through this world.

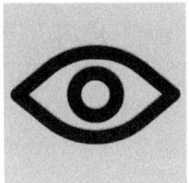

15

the Book of Perspectives

1 Consider, dear sojourner, how each person sees the world through different eyes. Like those standing at various points around a mountain, each one sees a real part of the mountain, but none sees the whole.

2 The Creator has placed each person at a unique vantage point. Your birth, your body, your experiences, your culture, your education, your joys and sufferings—all these shape how you see the world.

3 No sojourner possesses the complete view. Each has been given a partial perspective, valuable but incomplete. This is not a flaw but a design that calls us toward humility and community.

4 The sojourner who believes their view is the only valid

one walks in pride and misses the richer understanding that comes from many vantage points.

5 Look at how the four gospel writers told the story of Jesus. Matthew, Mark, Luke, and John each saw the same Lord but highlighted different aspects of his life and teachings. Together, they give us a fuller picture than any one alone could provide.

6 So it is with all important matters in life. Whether facing personal decisions, challenges, or seeking to understand truth, wisdom often emerges from considering multiple perspectives.

7 The wise sojourner neither dismisses all other viewpoints nor abandons their own unique insight. Instead, they learn to value both their perspective and the different angles from which others see.

8 For in the gathering of many perspectives, something greater than the sum of individual views can emerge—a wisdom that more closely approaches the whole truth that no single viewpoint can fully capture.

2 Each sojourner's view is shaped by many factors. Some you were born with, like your physical senses and natural temperament. Some came through your upbringing—the values taught by your family, the beliefs of your community, the experiences of your early years.

2 Other influences come through your chosen path—the knowledge you've sought, the people you've connected with, the places you've journeyed, the work you've done, and the hardships you've faced or avoided.

3 Consider how a person who grew up with plenty sees economic matters differently than one who knew poverty. How differently a person sees conflict if they experienced violence rather than peace in their formative years. How age, gender, health, education, and countless other factors color what each one sees.

4 This uniqueness is not random but purposeful. Your particular lens allows you to notice what others might miss. The insights that come naturally to you might be revelations to others.

5 The artist sees beauty where the engineer might see structure. The healer notices suffering where the teacher perceives a learning opportunity. The child often sees possibilities that adults have learned to overlook. None is wrong; each sees something real.

6 Therefore, do not apologize for your perspective as if it should match others exactly.

7 Your unique viewpoint is a gift, not just for you but for the wider community that needs the particular insight you alone might provide.

8 At times you will notice things others deny or dismiss. This does not automatically mean you are wrong. It may be that you are seeing something real that others cannot yet perceive from their position on the path.

9 The sojourner walking with humility neither abandons their unique perspective to blend with the crowd nor clings to it with rigid certainty that refuses to learn from others. Instead, they offer their view as one contribution to a greater understanding.

3 Yet while all perspectives offer some value, not all viewpoints are equally accurate, complete, or helpful. The wise sojourner learns to discern the difference between diverse viewpoints and distorted ones.

2 Some perspectives are tainted by wounds from the past. A person betrayed may see disloyalty everywhere. One who was neglected may interpret neutral actions as rejection. One who was praised only for achievement may view all relationships as transactions.

3 These distortions are not deliberate lies but genuine

perceptions shaped by painful experiences. The lens through which such sojourners view the world has been scratched or cracked, causing them to see patterns that may not truly exist in their present reality.

4 Other perspectives are limited by lack of experience or information. Those who have traveled only narrow paths may not comprehend the breadth of human reality. Those who have accessed only certain types of knowledge may draw conclusions based on partial information.

5 Still other viewpoints become clouded by what happens when sojourners gather in groups that think alike. In the comfort of agreement, critical thinking often weakens. Ideas go unchallenged. Opposing views are dismissed without fair consideration. Nuance disappears in favor of simplistic certainty.

6 This "group thinking" occurs in communities of all kinds—religious and secular, conservative and progressive, academic and practical.

7 When sojourners value belonging to the group more than seeking truth, perspectives narrow rather than expand.

8 Some of the most dangerous distortions come when perspectives are corrupted by pride, fear, or desire for power.

9 Those seeking to control others may deliberately twist reality. Those protecting their position may deny clear evidence. Those pursuing wealth or influence may blind themselves to the harm their path causes.

10 Remember that even a partially accurate perspective can lead to harmful conclusions when it claims to be the complete truth.

11 Much damage has been done by sojourners who correctly perceive one aspect of reality but fail to acknowledge the aspects they cannot see.

4 Given these limitations, how shall the sojourner determine which perspectives to trust more fully? By what measure

should viewpoints be evaluated? Here wisdom offers several guideposts.

2 Consider the fruits that grow from a particular perspective. Does this viewpoint lead toward love or division? Does it foster peace or constant conflict? Does it promote healing or ongoing harm? Does it encourage growth or stagnation?

3 By their fruits, perspectives can often be known.

4 Examine whether a viewpoint acknowledges its own limitations.

5 Those who claim to possess the complete and final truth on complex matters often hold distorted perspectives.

6 Those who admit the partial nature of their understanding tend to see more clearly.

7 Notice whether a perspective can incorporate new information and evolve over time. Rigid viewpoints that cannot adapt when faced with new evidence are less trustworthy than those flexible enough to grow and develop.

8 Be wary of perspectives that consistently position their holder as superior, exceptional, or uniquely victimized.

9 While each person's experience is valid, viewpoints that serve mainly to elevate the self or justify harm to others often contain significant distortion.

10 Consider the character and motives of those offering their perspective. Not to judge their worth as people, but to wisely evaluate how their position or interests might shape what they see or claim to see.

11 Pay attention to perspectives that have stood the test of time across many cultures. While age alone does not guarantee wisdom, viewpoints that have proven valuable to sojourners in many times and places often contain enduring truth.

12 Seek the guidance of the Spirit who leads toward truth. In quiet reflection, in prayer, in deep listening beyond surface reactions, discernment often comes.

13 The still, small voice that speaks in silence frequently offers clarity when competing perspectives create confusion.

5 Some sojourners, recognizing the value of many viewpoints and the limitations of each, fall into a different trap. Overwhelmed by competing perspectives, they become unable to form convictions or take action. This paralysis serves neither themselves nor others well.

2 They say, "Who can know what is truly right? There are so many views, all partial, all limited. Perhaps there is no solid ground on which to stand." And so they remain frozen, afraid to trust any perspective enough to move forward.

3 This approach seems humble but often hides a different kind of pride—the unwillingness to risk being wrong, the desire to remain above the messy work of discernment, the fear of responsibility that comes with making choices based on limited understanding.

4 Remember that the purpose of considering many perspectives is not to remain perpetually undecided but to gain a fuller understanding that informs wise action. The goal is not endless contemplation but more complete comprehension that leads to right living.

5 Even with limited sight, the sojourner must still navigate the path before them. Decisions must be made. Actions must be taken. Convictions must be formed. The question is not whether to proceed with partial understanding, but how to proceed wisely despite it.

6 Consider how the early church faced complex questions about including non-Jewish believers. They listened to many perspectives, weighed evidence from Scripture and experience, sought the Spirit's guidance, and then made decisions that shaped their community's path.

7 They did not claim perfect understanding, but neither did they use the complexity of the issue to avoid taking a

stand. They held their conclusions with both conviction and humility—firm enough to act upon, humble enough to adjust as new insight emerged.

8 The wise sojourner follows this pattern, neither rushing to judgment before considering diverse viewpoints nor using diversity as an excuse for endless indecision. They take the time needed for discernment, then move forward with both conviction and openness to growth.

6 How then shall the sojourner develop their own perspective with appropriate confidence? Not with rigid certainty that refuses correction, but with trust in their capacity to see truly, even if partially.

2 Know yourself and how your particular formation shapes what you see. Be honest about your biases, wounds, fears, and desires that might distort your vision. This self-awareness does not invalidate your perspective but clarifies its particular strengths and limitations.

3 Actively seek viewpoints different from your own, especially from those with different life experiences. Read widely, listen deeply, and engage respectfully with those who see differently. Let their perspectives challenge and enrich your own.

4 Find trustworthy companions for the journey—not those who merely confirm what you already believe, but those who share your commitment to truth and growth. Allow them to question your assumptions and point out your blind spots.

5 Develop the practice of stepping back from your immediate reactions. First impressions, while valuable, often reflect unconscious biases or triggered emotions. Give yourself time to move beyond initial responses to deeper understanding.

6 Continually expand your knowledge and experience. Travel new paths, learn new skills, expose yourself to

unfamiliar ideas. The broader your experience, the more complete your perspective becomes.

7 Remember that confidence grows through humble testing of your viewpoint, not through stubborn defense of it.

8 When you allow your perspective to be examined and find it holds up to scrutiny, genuine confidence emerges.

9 Trust the unique wisdom you have gained through your particular journey. No one else has lived your exact life or seen through your precise lens.

10 The insights that come most naturally to you are often the very gifts you are meant to contribute.

7 The mature sojourner eventually finds peace with the paradox of perspective—that we must live with conviction based on partial understanding, that we must act decisively while remaining open to correction, that we must trust our viewpoint while recognizing its limitations.

2 This is not weakness but wisdom. It is not indecision but discernment. It is not doubt but humble confidence that distinguishes between what we know with certainty and what we hold as probable or possible.

3 Consider the example of the apostle Paul, who wrote, "Now I know in part; then I shall know fully." Yet this acknowledgment of partial understanding did not prevent him from proclaiming truth with conviction or making difficult decisions that shaped the early church.

4 The sojourner grows in the ability to say both "This is what I see clearly" and "I may be missing something important." Both "These are the convictions by which I live" and "I remain open to deeper understanding."

5 This balanced approach allows for strong commitment without rigid dogmatism. It enables meaningful action without the paralysis of perfect certainty. It fosters both conviction and continuous learning.

6 When you encounter perspectives that differ from yours, neither automatically dismiss them nor automatically abandon your own viewpoint. Instead, ask: What might be true in this different perspective? What might the other person be seeing that I have missed? How might this viewpoint complement or correct my own?

7 At the same time, honor the unique perspective you have developed through your life experience, learning, and spiritual insight.

8 Your viewpoint matters not just for you but for others who need what you have seen and understood.

9 Remember that no individual sojourner is meant to see everything. Our limited perspectives are not a flaw in creation but an invitation to community, where different viewpoints come together to create a more complete understanding than any one person could develop alone.

10 Walk, then, with both conviction and humility. Speak what you see with clarity and courage. Listen to others with genuine openness. Hold your perspective as a valuable gift to be offered, not an absolute truth to be imposed.

11 For in the end, all sojourners "see through a glass, darkly" during this earthly journey. One day, perspective will give way to full understanding. Until then, we walk by faith, not by sight—yet not blindly, but with the partial yet real light given to each of us to share with others.

16

the Book of Shadows

1 As we travel through this world, we encounter not only beauty, goodness, and light, but also darkness, evil, and shadow.

2 This darkness shows itself most clearly through fellow sojourners who have turned toward destruction, negativity, and selfishness at the expense of others.

3 Some embrace darkness willingly, choosing paths of control, exploitation, and cruelty with full awareness.

4 They seek power over others rather than connection with them, gathering for themselves rather than growth for all, and satisfying their desires regardless of the cost to others.

5 Some serve darkness unknowingly, believing themselves righteous while causing harm.

6 Blinded by fear, ideology, or false certainty, they destroy what is good while calling it evil, harm those they claim to help, and create suffering while pursuing what they believe is right.

7 Some spread darkness through action—violence that wounds bodies, exploitation that depletes resources, words that destroy reputations, systems that oppress the vulnerable.

8 Others spread it through inaction—standing silent in the face of injustice, turning away from suffering they could help, refusing responsibility for harm they could prevent.

9 We cannot avoid encounters with such darkness. It appears on highways and in centers, in seats of power and in ordinary homes, in distant lands and in neighbors.

10 Sometimes darkness appears even in the mirror, when we ourselves turn from our true path toward destructive ways.

11 This reality raises deep questions for the journey: How shall we live in a world where such darkness exists? How shall we respond when darkness crosses our path? How shall we protect our own light without extinguishing it through fear, hatred, or revenge?

12 These questions have no simple answers, for evil is complex in its origins and expressions.

13 Yet we cannot ignore them, for how we respond to darkness shapes our entire journey—either strengthening our authentic path or pulling us toward the very darkness we oppose.

14 The sojourner who learns to navigate darkness without being consumed by it discovers a form of strength that those who know only light cannot possess—the strength that comes from choosing light precisely because they understand the reality of darkness.

2 Before determining how to live amid darkness, we must understand its nature.

2 For darkness is not a simple thing, and responses based on misunderstanding often increase rather than reduce its power.

3 Darkness is real but not ultimate.

4 The evil that humans do causes genuine suffering that cannot be dismissed as illusion or explained away.

5 Yet evil is not equal in power to goodness, not an eternal principle opposed to light, but rather a distortion and rejection of the good that remains the fundamental reality.

6 Darkness thrives through disconnection. When humans lose sight of their fundamental interdependence, when they forget their common origin in the Creator, when they fail to see themselves in others and others in themselves—in this forgetting, the seeds of evil find fertile ground.

7 No one is immune to darkness.

8 The capacity for harm lies within each sojourner. Given certain conditions—extreme fear, intense pain, early trauma, gradual corruption, or persistent deception—anyone might turn toward destructive paths.

9 This truth calls for humility rather than self-righteousness when facing others' failings.

10 Darkness often disguises itself as light.

11 Those who work greatest harm frequently believe themselves justified, even heroic in their actions.

12 Evil rarely presents itself nakedly but cloaks itself in noble purposes, righteous anger, or necessary means to worthy ends.

13 Some people have given themselves so completely to darkness that they become, in essence, vessels of evil itself. These are not merely confused or wounded people who cause harm unknowingly, but those who have repeatedly chosen destruction until it has consumed their very nature. Such sojourners cannot be "fixed" or reformed through human efforts alone, regardless of compassion offered or

consequences imposed. Their redemption, if it comes, lies solely in the hands of the Creator.

14 While some have fully embraced darkness, many others who cause harm do so not because they love evil but because they see too narrowly, feel too desperately, or know too incompletely to recognize the damage they create. Telling the difference between these categories requires wisdom beyond simple judgment.

15 In light of these truths, we approach darkness with neither naive dismissal nor paralyzing dread, but with clear-eyed recognition of its reality, complexity, and limitations.

16 We neither underestimate its destructive potential nor grant it more power than it actually possesses.

17 Understanding darkness accurately becomes the foundation for maintaining hope—not hope based on denial of evil's reality, but hope grounded in recognition that darkness, however powerful, cannot extinguish the light that is woven into the very fabric of existence.

3 When darkness shows itself through destructive, negative, and selfish actions, it affects our journey in profound ways that cannot be ignored or minimized.

2 Darkness brings tangible suffering—physical pain, material deprivation, loss of security and wellbeing.

3 When one person exploits another, when systems oppress the vulnerable, when violence erupts between peoples, real wounds are inflicted on real bodies and communities.

4 Darkness brings psychological distress—fear that limits possibility, grief that drains energy, confusion that clouds judgment, trauma that fragments experience. These inner wounds can persist long after external circumstances change, altering how we perceive and navigate our path.

5 Darkness brings spiritual challenges—anger that hardens the heart, bitterness that poisons relationships, despair that

questions meaning, cynicism that rejects hope. These spiritual poisons can gradually transform us until we no longer recognize our own face in clear mirrors.

6 Darkness brings ethical dilemmas—how to respond to aggression without becoming aggressive, how to resist injustice without creating new injustice, how to protect the vulnerable without dehumanizing the perpetrator, how to speak truth without weaponizing it.

7 The impact of darkness is not distributed equally among people. Some bear greater burdens of suffering due to where and to whom they were born, what resources they can access, or what powers are arrayed against them.

8 Yet no one escapes darkness entirely. Even those most protected by privilege, power, or geography cannot fully protect themselves from the reality of evil and its effects.

9 For we are all connected, and the suffering of any part eventually reaches the whole.

10 Yet even in acknowledging darkness's real impact, we must remember that its effects, while genuine, are not permanent or total. Wounds can heal, trauma can be processed, and systems can be changed. The very fact that we can recognize and name darkness's effects means we retain the capacity to address them.

11 Those who have endured the deepest darkness often develop the greatest capacity for light—not despite their suffering but because of how they chose to respond to it. This is not a justification for evil but a testimony to the indomitable nature of the human spirit.

4 Throughout history, people have developed many responses to the darkness they encounter. Some of these responses, though common, ultimately fail to address evil adequately or lead us away from our authentic path.

2 There is the response of denial—refusing to see evil

that is plainly present, explaining away cruelty as misunderstanding, calling exploitation by more acceptable names. This response fails because what we do not acknowledge, we cannot address.

3 What remains in shadow grows stronger, not weaker.

4 There is the response of despair—concluding that darkness is too powerful to resist, that evil will always triumph, that working for good is futile. This response grants darkness more power than it possesses.

5 Light, though sometimes dimmed, cannot be extinguished.

6 There is the response of naivety—believing that all who do evil can be reformed through sufficient understanding, compassion, or therapeutic intervention.

7 While many who cause harm can indeed change, this response fails to recognize that some have so thoroughly embraced darkness that their redemption lies beyond human capacity and belongs solely to the Creator.

8 There is also the overzealous response of demonization—seeing all those who do evil as wholly other, as monsters rather than fellow humans, assuming that all who cause harm are irredeemably evil rather than discerning between those who might change and those who will not.

9 Demonization often leads to committing new wrongs in the name of fighting wrong.

10 There is the response of division—separating the world neatly into good people and bad people, righteous nations and evil nations, good beliefs and wicked beliefs. This response oversimplifies the mixture of light and shadow present in most people, communities, and traditions, while failing to acknowledge that true evil does exist in some.

11 There is the response of domination—attempting to overcome evil through greater force, superior violence, more effective control. This response often adopts the very methods

of darkness while claiming to fight it, creating cycles of harm that perpetuate rather than heal brokenness.

12 There is the response of disengagement—withdrawing from the world's pain, creating private sanctuaries of comfort, focusing only on personal spiritual development while ignoring collective suffering.

13 Isolation is not innocence.

14 The absence of conflict is not the presence of peace.

15 The person who wishes to travel wisely must recognize these false responses when they arise within themselves or their communities, understanding that each represents an understandable but ultimately inadequate reaction to the genuine challenge of evil.

16 Recognizing these inadequate responses is itself a form of hope, for it means that better responses exist. The very fact that we can identify what doesn't work points toward what might work better.

5 How then shall we live in a world where darkness manifests through willing and unwitting harm? These practices offer wisdom for the journey through shadow while maintaining connection to light.

2 Cultivate clear seeing. We must develop the capacity to look directly at evil without turning away in denial or being overwhelmed by despair. This clear seeing acknowledges darkness where it exists, light that remains, goodness that persists, and beauty that continues to emerge even in difficult terrain.

3 Clear seeing includes recognizing the small lights that shine even in the darkest places—the nurse who tends the dying with compassion, the teacher who refuses to give up on difficult students, the neighbor who checks on the elderly during storms.

4 Maintain a stance of active hope. Unlike blind

optimism that denies problems or passive pessimism that surrenders to them, active hope acknowledges difficulty while committing to possibility.

5 Hope works for good outcomes without attaching its worth to immediate results.

6 Setbacks are not final defeats.

7 Apparent failures prepare the ground for future possibilities.

8 Active hope remembers that every great achievement in human history began with someone refusing to accept that the current darkness was permanent. The abolition of slavery, the advancement of human rights, the development of medicines that save lives—all emerged from people who maintained hope despite overwhelming darkness.

9 Practice discerning resistance. We must oppose evil, but how this opposition is implemented requires wisdom. Sometimes resistance means direct confrontation. Sometimes it means creating alternatives. Sometimes it means bearing witness to suffering. Sometimes it means healing wounds. The path of wisdom discerns which response serves light in each particular circumstance.

10 Resistance itself becomes a form of hope—not just the hope that evil can be defeated, but the hope demonstrated through the very act of refusing to accept evil as inevitable.

11 Develop wise discernment. We must distinguish between those who do harm but remain capable of change and those who have become so thoroughly corrupted that their redemption lies beyond human capacity. This discernment—neither naively assuming all can be changed nor hastily judging all wrongdoers as irredeemable—requires deep wisdom, careful observation, and spiritual insight.

12 For those truly given to evil, we recognize that ultimate justice and possible redemption belong to the Creator alone.

13 Remember common humanity. When opposing the

harmful actions of others, we maintain awareness of shared humanity with most who do harm. This does not mean excusing wrong or bypassing accountability, but recognizing that demonizing others reduces our own humanity and perpetuates cycles of dehumanization that feed darkness.

14 Even with those who have fully embraced evil, we remember that they too were once created in divine image, however distorted that image has become.

15 This memory of shared humanity becomes itself a form of resistance against darkness, refusing to let evil reduce our own capacity for seeing the human in others.

16 Protect but do not close the heart. We develop healthy boundaries that prevent unnecessary harm while avoiding the fortress mentality that confuses safety with isolation.

17 The open heart is vulnerable but necessary; the closed heart is protected but deadened. Wisdom finds the middle path that allows connection without unnecessary suffering.

18 An open but protected heart maintains the capacity to love even while refusing to be victimized—perhaps the greatest victory over darkness available to human beings.

19 Commit to healing justice. We work not merely to punish those who do harm but to repair what has been broken, restore what has been damaged, and create conditions where healing becomes possible.

20 Justice seeks not vengeance but transformation—the reweaving of torn fabric rather than its further shredding.

21 Yet we also accept that some who do evil remain beyond human rehabilitation, and in such cases, justice may focus more on protection and containment than transformation.

22 Healing justice carries within it the hope that broken systems can be repaired, wounded communities can recover, and even perpetrators of harm can sometimes find paths to redemption.

23 Practice presence with suffering. We develop the capacity to be fully present with pain—our own and others'—without either drowning in it or shutting down to it. This presence does not magically remove suffering but prevents it from having the final word.

24 The ability to be present with suffering without being destroyed by it becomes a form of hope in action—demonstrating that pain, while real, need not be permanently destructive.

6 As we encounter external darkness, we must also attend to the shadows that arise within. For outer evil often triggers inner responses that can either clarify or distort our path.

2 Be attentive to reactive anger. When witnessing cruelty or injustice, righteous anger naturally arises. It can fuel necessary action but also can consume us from within if not consciously held.

3 The wise sojourner neither suppresses this anger nor is controlled by it, but channels its energy toward constructive response.

4 Be attentive to fear's distortions. When facing threat, fear narrows perception, amplifies danger, and activates ancient survival responses. These reactions served our ancestors well against predators but often misguide us in complex human conflicts.

5 We acknowledge fear without allowing it to dictate our understanding or response.

6 Be attentive to the desire for certainty. When confronting evil's complexity, the mind seeks the comfort of absolute clarity about who is right and who is wrong, what is good and what is bad.

7 Knowing is necessary, but rigid certainty blinds us to nuance, context, and the mixture of motives present in human affairs.

8 Be attentive to the impulse toward hatred. When repeatedly harmed or threatened, the heart may harden toward those perceived as enemies. This hardening feels like strength but actually takes away from us, cutting us off from our full humanity.

9 Hatred binds you to those you hate through negative attachment.

10 Be attentive to the shadow within. The evil we most readily recognize and condemn in others often reflects hidden aspects of ourselves. We develop the courage to examine our own capacity for harm, our own destructive impulses, our own selfishness disguised as goodness.

11 Self-examination brings not self-condemnation but greater wholeness and humility.

12 This inner work is not separate from addressing external darkness but essential to it. The person who neglects their inner self while fighting outer evil often recreates the very patterns they oppose.

13 The one who tends their own garden of consciousness cultivates growth.

7 As we travel through land darkened by destruction, negativity, and selfishness, we may question: Where is the Creator in this shadowed world? Has divine presence withdrawn from these broken places? Must I walk alone through valleys of death and despair?

2 The divine light shines even in the darkest places, though sometimes it appears only as the faintest glimmer rather than brilliant illumination.

3 The Creator has not abandoned even the most damaged landscapes of human experience.

4 Divine presence manifests in unexpected courage that arises amid fear, in resilience that presents during trauma, in compassion that emerges from suffering, in clarity that comes

through confusion, in connection that forms within brokenness.

5 Divine presence appears in moments when enemies see each other's humanity, when the wounded find a voice to speak their truth, when the privileged awaken to others' pain, when the weak find strength to choose a different path.

6 Divine presence works through the person who chooses love when hate seems more justified, who maintains integrity when corruption offers easier passage, who speaks truth when lies promise greater rewards, who extends compassion when indifference would be simpler.

7 Divine presence remains even in the face of those who have given themselves fully to evil—not in their actions, which oppose divine nature, but in the Creator's continued authority over all existence.

8 For while some have placed themselves beyond human redemption, no one lies beyond the reach of divine power.

9 What appears impossible for human effort remains possible for the Creator, who alone can transform what is truly evil into what is good.

10 Even in the darkest night of evil, when no light seems visible, the divine remains present—not as magic that instantly removes suffering, not as power that violates human freedom, but as the golden thread of love and possibility that runs through all reality, and as the ultimate authority to which all beings are finally accountable.

11 The person who attunes to this thread finds not immunity from darkness but a deeper resilience within it.

12 While evil can wound the body, disrupt communities, and challenge beliefs, it cannot ultimately separate the human spirit from divine presence unless we ourselves choose to let go.

13 Evil, however powerful it appears, cannot escape the final justice of the Creator.

14 This understanding becomes a source of unshakeable hope—not hope that all evil will be defeated in our lifetime, but hope that evil will never have the final word, that love is the ultimate reality, that the arc of existence bends toward justice even when we cannot see its curve.

15 Recognizing divine presence in dark places transforms how we engage with darkness. We work against evil not from desperation but from confidence, not from fear but from love, not as those who must single-handedly save the world but as those who participate in a larger work of redemption.

8 As we continue our journey through shadow lands, facing both external evil and internal reactions with clarity and compassion, a paradoxical truth gradually emerges: Darkness, while never good in itself, can become an occasion for transformation.

2 The encounter with evil, while painful, often strips away illusions about human nature, social systems, and even our own character. This stripping, though uncomfortable, creates space for more authentic understanding and connection with reality as it is rather than as we wish it to be.

3 The experience of suffering, while never desirable, frequently deepens the capacity for empathy with others who suffer. Hearts broken open by pain become more able to understand others' struggles without turning away or shutting down.

4 The confrontation with injustice, while distressing, commonly awakens commitment to creating more just alternatives. Many movements for healing have emerged precisely from those who experienced or witnessed harm and refused to accept it as inevitable.

5 The recognition of accepting harmful systems, while shameful, often creates more conscious choices about how to live. Awakening to one's participation in damage creates

possibility for participation in repair that was not available during unconsciousness.

6 The acknowledgment of inner shadow, while humbling, usually enables more honesty and compassion with others' failings.

7 The person who has faced their own capacity for harm becomes less judgmental of others' wrongdoing without minimizing its effects.

8 These transformations do not justify or redeem evil itself. Destruction remains destruction, harm remains harm, suffering remains suffering—yet the human ability to grow through darkness rather than being destroyed by it hints at a deeper pattern woven into the fabric of reality.

9 This pattern suggests that while darkness has genuine power to wound, it does not have ultimate power to determine our journey.

10 The final word belongs not to evil but to the possibility of transformation that persists even in the darkest places.

11 This recognition becomes a profound source of hope —not hope that evil is really good in disguise, but hope that good can emerge from evil, that meaning can be wrested from meaninglessness, that even the worst experiences can be transformed into sources of wisdom and compassion.

12 Those who work with trauma survivors witness this daily—how people who have endured unimaginable darkness often develop extraordinary capacity for healing others. This is not because suffering is good, but because humans have remarkable ability to transform suffering into service.

13 History provides countless examples of this transformative possibility—former slaves who became abolitionists, holocaust survivors who devoted their lives to preventing genocide, former addicts who become counselors, victims of abuse who become advocates for justice.

14 Recognizing this possibility does not minimize the

reality of evil or suggest that victims are responsible for finding meaning in their suffering. But it does offer hope that evil, while powerful, is not the end of the story.

15 Therefore, let us travel with soberness of evil's reality, clear-eyed resistance to its destructive force, and genuine compassion for its victims and perpetrators alike—while maintaining unshakable trust that light, though sometimes dim, remains the fundamental truth of existence toward which all journeys ultimately go.

16 This hope is not naive because it acknowledges evil's genuine power. This hope is not passive because it calls us to active resistance. This hope is not individual because it connects us to all who work for justice. This hope is not temporary because it is grounded in the eternal nature of love itself.

17 In this hope, we find the strength to continue working for good even when progress seems impossible, to maintain compassion even when surrounded by cruelty, to keep building even when destruction appears to be winning.

18 For we know that every act of kindness matters, every word of truth has power, every moment of genuine connection creates light that darkness cannot extinguish.

19 And in this work, we discover that engaging with darkness does not require becoming dark ourselves, that fighting evil does not require abandoning good, that maintaining hope in the face of evil is not naivety but the deepest form of wisdom and courage available to human beings.

17

the Book of Freedom

1 Consider how people seek freedom in this world. Many travel endlessly, always searching for escape from what binds them, yet finding themselves more tightly trapped with each attempt to flee.

2 See the great paradox that faces every sojourner on the path to freedom: the very act of trying to be free from something plants that very thing more firmly in your heart and mind.

3 Like someone caught in quicksand who struggles violently to escape, only to sink more quickly into its depths, so too does the person who focuses on breaking free from their burdens often find themselves more completely defined by them.

4 For what fills your thoughts controls your journey.

5 What you run from chases you.

6 What you resist, persists.

7 The thing you hate, though you turn away from it, secretly guides your steps.

8 Think about how a person determined not to think about something finds their mind filled with it. The command "Don't think about this" ensures it becomes the focus of all thinking.

9 So it is with the burdens we carry—our struggles, our weaknesses, our repeating patterns. The more desperately we seek freedom from them, the more firmly they establish themselves in our inner rooms.

10 Like a trap that tightens with each attempt to pull away, our struggles intensify the more we seek escape. Our very attempt at freedom becomes another form of bondage.

11 Even in our deepest practices—meditation, therapy, self-help—many find this pattern continues. They release their burdens in one moment, only to take them back in the next, now heavier for having been briefly set down.

12 Thus begins a cycle of frustration, anger, and discouragement that leaves us weary and defeated, feeling like failures on the journey, unworthy of the freedom we seek.

2 Notice how many institutions and people thrive on this dynamic, creating systems where guilt and shame becomes the main currency of exchange.

2 Not through evil intent or conscious design do they keep this cycle going, but through unconscious following of patterns that maintain their authority, control and purpose in people's lives.

3 For as long as people walk in guilt and shame, they will need guides who offer paths to healing, teachers who explain right from wrong, authorities who maintain standards, and sanctuaries where redemption can be performed.

4 Thus, many institutions become marketplaces where guilt and shame are exchanged for temporary relief, only for the cycle to begin again the next day.

5 The institutions create standards and measures by which people can validate their identity as worthy members. Not requirements for belonging, but benchmarks for proving one is actually a "good" person.

6 Those who love power, who crave respect, or who fear the unknown direction that true freedom might take, often become the strongest defenders of these systems, though they themselves may not recognize the true nature of their resistance.

7 Within these structures, the message of complete freedom—the true heart of human liberation—remains buried beneath layers of tradition and misunderstanding, rarely proclaimed with the energy reserved for more comfortable messages.

8 Yet there have always been those, such as the Apostle Paul, who glimpsed and taught a more radical vision of freedom, though their words were often misunderstood, their teachings frequently distorted by those who could not understand nor accept their revolutionary nature.

3 Consider the words of great teachers throughout history who declared radical freedom from the chains of guilt and shame.

2 The philosopher who said, "All things are within human capacity, but not all things serve human growth." And again: "The positive law of growth and what is best has set you free from the law of rules, stagnation and decline."

3 These are not the teachings of someone who promotes a restrictive, rule-bound life, but the proclamations of one who has glimpsed a radical new way of living, a freedom so complete that its implications inspire both wonder and fear.

4 For such teachers proclaimed that we can be released from the patterns that bind us, so that just as life itself continually regenerates, we too might walk in newness of being.

5 And they declared: "Guilt and shame will have no power over you, since you are not under rigid systems of rules and negativity, but under natural flow of growth and positivity." And again: "Now we are released from the old patterns, having died to what held us captive, so that we serve in the new way of authentic living which looks for the best way and not in the old way of imposed codes which says, "You cannot"."

6 This message represents a transformation of cosmic proportions for the sojourner. It proclaims a freedom that goes beyond the world's false versions—the endless cycles of shame and temporary relief, the constant demand for external validation, the belief that liberty means doing whatever one desires without consequences.

7 True freedom is a life lived beyond rigid rules, imposed expectations, others' opinions, perfectionist standards, guilt and shame, and even the need to prove one's worth.

8 In its brilliant light, concepts of inadequacy, imposed law, externally-defined morality, shame and self-punishment have died and become useless shadows—nonexistent for the truly free person.

9 Yet this freedom is total, absolute, and transformative not because it is freedom from something, but because it is freedom for something. This subtle shift in perspective changes everything on the sojourner's path.

10 The question is no longer, "Why can't I be free from this burden?" but "Why are we given such radical freedom? What purpose does it serve?"

11 The answer reveals itself: We are set free so that we can follow the guidance of our deepest wisdom and voice without hindrance.

4 We discover the depths of our freedom when we shift our focus from asking life to free us from our struggles and

instead ask to be freed for the purpose of following our authentic nature.

2 This key change moves attention away from personal inadequacies and places it squarely on natural strength and inner guidance. As a result, we find that our authentic power perfectly overcomes learned limitations.

3 Many people, granted complete freedom by life itself, choose to stay in familiar confinement rather than step into the unknown expanse of true freedom.

4 Why do we cling to chains when the cell door stands wide open?

5 Perhaps because true freedom carries with it great responsibility.

6 It is easier, in many ways, to live by someone else's rules, to have paths clearly marked, to give up the burden of choice.

7 For freedom requires us to think deeply, to make difficult choices, to bear the weight of our own decisions.

8 There is comfort in constraint that makes bondage sometimes seem preferable to freedom.

9 Yet here emerges another paradox: in choosing to follow the guidance of our deepest wisdom, we find ourselves freer than we could ever be by following our immediate impulses. It is a freedom that liberates not just from external constraints, but from our own self-destructive tendencies.

10 This freedom enables us to love without fear, to serve without resentment, to give without expectation of return.

11 Freedom makes possible the forgiveness of the unforgivable, the discovery of joy amid sorrow, the experience of peace that surpasses understanding even when storms rage.

12 It transforms us from within, ensuring we are no longer defined by past mistakes, current struggles, or others' expectations.

13 Instead, our identity rests securely in being authentic expressions of life itself, empowered by our deepest wisdom.

5 This freedom is not permission to follow every impulse, but power to become what we were born to be.

2 It is the liberty to live out our authentic purpose without the constraints of fear, shame, or the need for constant approval.

3 In this new light, even struggles and challenges take on a different meaning. They are no longer obstacles to overcome or burdens to escape, but opportunities for growth, chances to experience natural resilience in human vulnerability, avenues for light to shine through brokenness.

4 The path to embracing this freedom is not always easy. It requires us to release our need for control, to trust wisdom deeper than our conscious mind. It demands steps beyond comfort, risks taken, living by inner guidance rather than external validation.

5 Yet the rewards surpass anything we could ask or imagine. Our journey becomes marked by love, joy, peace, patience, kindness, goodness, faithfulness, gentleness, and authentic confidence—not because we strive to follow rules, but because these qualities naturally flow from a heart set free.

6 This freedom transforms how we view fellow sojourners. No longer burdened by the need to prove our worth or earn our place, we can love others without agenda, extend grace because we have received grace, forgive because we understand the universal nature of human limitation, accept others as they are because we have learned to accept ourselves as we are.

7 The impact of this freedom ripples outward, touching every aspect of our life and the lives of those we encounter.

8 Freedom holds power to transform not just individuals but families, communities, and even entire societies.

9 Living in this freedom begins with a choice—to believe we are truly free, to step out of self-imposed prisons into the

wide-open spaces of authentic living, to listen for the gentle whisper of our deepest wisdom and follow where it leads.

10 It means releasing the need to earn love or prove our worth, embracing identity as authentic expressions of life itself not because of what we have accomplished but because of the inherent value of existence, living from a place of acceptance rather than striving for acceptance.

6 This freedom gives us courage to take risks, to step out in faith, to dream big dreams and pursue authentic passions.

2 It empowers us to live with radical generosity, scandalous forgiveness, and unlimited love. These qualities emerge not from obligation or fear, but as natural expressions of a freed heart.

3 Perhaps most significantly, this freedom transforms our relationship with the deeper mysteries of existence. We can approach not as trembling servants fearful of punishment, but as authentic beings secure in our inherent worth, confident in the natural flow of life.

4 The free person can be honest about struggles, doubts, and fears, knowing that nothing can separate them from their fundamental value as conscious beings.

5 There is no need to hide or pretend, to perform or impress.

6 This is the freedom proclaimed by wisdom traditions throughout history, the liberation that has the power to break every chain of shame and fear. As it was written: "There is therefore now no condemnation for those who live authentically."

7 The person who grasps this truth discovers that freedom is not primarily about what one is freed from, but what one is freed for. Not escape, but purpose. Not merely the absence of constraint, but the presence of possibility.

8 So let us not focus on fleeing what binds us, but on embracing what awaits us. Not on breaking chains, but on

building new realities. Not on what lies behind, but on what lies ahead.

9 For true freedom—this active, ongoing state of living in liberation—comes not when we finally escape all that troubles us, but when we live fully for the purpose to which our authentic nature calls us, guided by our deepest wisdom, secure in worth that cannot be earned and cannot be lost.

7 We discover the depths of our freedom when we understand that the struggle itself often points the way to liberation.

2 What we resist most strongly often contains the energy we need for transformation, like coal that becomes diamond under pressure.

3 The patterns we fight against may be calling our attention to aspects of ourselves that need integration rather than elimination.

4 Consider how the person who struggles with anger may need to learn healthy boundaries, how the one who battles anxiety may need to develop trust in their own resilience.

5 Freedom comes not from defeating these patterns but from understanding their message and transforming their energy toward constructive purpose.

6 The recovering addict who becomes a counselor, the trauma survivor who becomes a healer, the anxious person who becomes a compassionate helper—these show us how struggles can become sources of strength.

7 This is the recipe of authentic freedom: exchanging the lead weight of our struggles into the valuable gold of wisdom and service.

8 When we stop fighting our patterns and start learning from them, we discover that every limitation contains information about our next step toward growth.

9 The prison becomes a classroom, the burden

becomes a teacher, the weakness becomes a doorway to unexpected strength.

8 True freedom also requires releasing the need to be understood or approved of by others in our choices.

2 Many people remain trapped not by external circumstances but by their attachment to others' opinions about their decisions.

3 They sacrifice their authentic path to maintain relationships that require them to be someone they are not.

4 But freedom means being willing to be misunderstood by those who cannot see your vision, criticized by those who fear change, or rejected by those who need you to stay small.

5 This does not mean becoming callous or indifferent to others, but rather recognizing that your first responsibility is to your own authentic unfolding.

6 When you live freely, you model possibility for others. Your courage to be yourself gives others permission to do the same.

7 The person who breaks free from family patterns of dysfunction, who chooses a different career than expected, who lives according to their values rather than others' expectations—they create new templates for what is possible.

8 Your freedom becomes a gift to the world, showing that change is possible, that authentic living is achievable, that people are not doomed to repeat old patterns forever.

9 Freedom ultimately means taking full responsibility for your own experience while releasing the need to control others' experiences.

2 You become free when you realize that your happiness does not depend on others' behavior, your peace does not require others' approval, your worth does not fluctuate based on others' treatment of you.

3 This recognition simultaneously empowers and humbles—empowers because you discover your ability to create your own inner conditions, humbles because you must release the illusion that you can create others' inner conditions.

4 Free people do not try to change others but rather focus their energy on their own growth and contribution.

5 They offer their gifts without demanding they be received, speak their truth without requiring it be accepted, love without needing that love to be returned.

6 This is the paradox of freedom: the less you need from others, the more you have to offer them. The less you demand from life, the more life gives you.

7 When you are truly free, relationships become opportunities for mutual growth rather than transactions for getting needs met.

8 Work becomes expression of purpose rather than just means of survival. Challenges become adventures rather than threats.

10 The journey to freedom is not a destination but a daily practice of choosing authenticity over approval, truth over comfort, growth over safety.

2 Each day offers new opportunities to practice freedom—in small choices to speak honestly, in decisions to follow your inner guidance rather than external pressure, in moments when you choose love over fear.

3 Freedom is built through these small acts of courage, like a muscle that grows stronger with regular exercise.

4 The person who practices freedom in small matters develops the strength to choose freedom in larger ones.

5 They learn that the temporary discomfort of authentic choice leads to lasting satisfaction, while the temporary comfort of inauthentic choice leads to lasting regret.

6 Begin where you are, with the choices available to you

today. Practice saying no to what does not serve your authentic path. Practice saying yes to what calls to your deepest values.

7 Notice how freedom feels in your body—the lightness that comes from honesty, the energy that flows from authentic action, the peace that follows alignment with your true nature.

8 Let these feelings guide you toward more freedom, using your body's wisdom as a compass for authentic living.

11 As you grow in freedom, you will face the temptation to use your liberation to judge or control others who have not yet chosen the same path.

2 This is the shadow side of freedom—the tendency to become prideful about your growth, impatient with others' struggles, or evangelical about your particular path to liberation.

3 True freedom includes the humility to remember that everyone finds their way in their own time, through their own experiences, according to their own readiness.

4 Your role is not to free others but to be free yourself, not to convince others of your path but to walk your path with integrity.

5 When you try to force your freedom on others, you abandon your own freedom and become enslaved to their response.

6 The truly free person remains compassionate toward those still in bondage, knowing that their own liberation came through struggle and often required multiple attempts.

7 They offer their example as inspiration, not their judgment as condemnation.

8 They remember that freedom is a gift to be shared, not a weapon to be wielded.

12 In the end, freedom is both the simplest and most complex truth: you are already free, and you must choose that freedom moment by moment.

2 You were born free, before conditioning taught you to be enslaved. You remain free, despite the patterns that seem to bind you. You will die free, regardless of the circumstances that surround your departure.

3 The prison exists only in your mind. The chains are made only of thoughts. The guards are only your own fears.

4 Yet choosing freedom requires everything you have—courage to face what you have avoided, honesty to see what you have denied, commitment to change what you have accepted.

5 Freedom is your birthright and your responsibility, your gift and your challenge, your deepest nature and your daily choice.

6 The door to freedom is always open. The key is always in your hand. The path is always available.

7 What remains is simply this: the choice to walk through the door, to use the key, to take the path.

8 To say, with full awareness of both the cost and the gift: "I choose freedom. I choose authenticity. I choose to be who I truly am."

9 This is the great work of a human life—not to achieve freedom someday, but to recognize and live the freedom that is already yours.

10 For you are free, have always been free, and the only question that remains is whether you will choose to live that freedom today.

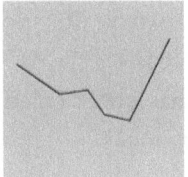

18

the Book of 𝔉ailure

1 Consider this truth that every sojourner on life's journey must face: failure is not the exception to human experience but its most reliable companion.

2 From the moment we take our first unsteady steps as children, stumbling and falling countless times before we learn to walk, failure walks beside us as teacher, corrector, and unexpected guide.

3 Yet most people spend their entire journey trying to avoid this faithful companion, seeing failure as enemy rather than instructor, as proof of weakness rather than evidence of effort.

4 They build their lives around the impossible goal of never falling, never making mistakes, never choosing wrongly —and in doing so, they often fail to live at all.

5 The wise sojourner learns a different relationship with failure, understanding that mistakes are not detours from the path but essential parts of the journey itself.

6 For how else would we learn what works if we never discover what doesn't? How would we develop resilience if we never faced setbacks? How would we appreciate success if we never had disappointment?

7 Failure is not the opposite of success but its prerequisite, not the absence of progress but proof that progress is being attempted.

8 The person who has never failed has simply never tried anything worth failing at.

2 Understand the crucial difference between failing and being a failure—between experiencing setbacks and allowing setbacks to define who you are.

2 To fail is to attempt something and not achieve the desired outcome. This is a temporary condition, a single event, a moment in time that provides information about what doesn't work.

3 To be a failure is to let that temporary condition become a permanent identity, to conclude that because you failed at something, you are fundamentally flawed or incapable.

4 The person who fails says, "This approach didn't work. Let me try something different." The person who identifies as a failure says, "I am broken. There's no point in trying."

5 Consider the child learning to ride a bicycle. They fall dozens of times, scraping knees and bruising elbows. But they don't conclude they are "a failure at transportation"—they simply get back on the bike and try again.

6 Somewhere along the journey to adulthood, many people lose this natural resilience, allowing individual failures to become evidence of personal inadequacy rather than information for improvement.

7 They forget that every expert was once a beginner, every master was once a disaster, every success story is built on a foundation of failures that taught essential lessons.

8 The surgeon who saves lives today once made clumsy cuts on practice dummies. The teacher who inspires students today once gave lessons that fell flat. The artist whose work moves hearts today once created pieces that satisfied no one.

9 Their current competence did not arise despite their past failures but because of them—each mistake providing feedback that guided them toward better performance.

3 Failure serves the sojourner's journey in ways that success alone never could, offering gifts that can be found nowhere else along the path.

2 Failure teaches humility when pride threatens to make you arrogant. Nothing deflates an inflated ego quite like a well-timed setback that reminds you of your limitations.

3 Failure develops empathy when judgment threatens to make you harsh toward others who struggle. Once you have felt the sting of your own mistakes, you become more compassionate toward others in their difficulties.

4 Failure builds resilience when comfort threatens to make you weak. The muscles of persistence and determination grow strong only through resistance, only by pushing through difficulty rather than around it.

5 Failure clarifies values when distraction threatens to lead you astray. Often it is only when pursuing the wrong things leads to disappointment that we discover what truly matters to us.

6 Failure forces creativity when routine threatens to make you stagnant. When the familiar approaches stop working, you must innovate, adapt, and discover new ways forward.

7 Failure provides perspective when temporary setbacks threaten to seem permanent. Each time you survive what felt

like disaster, you gain confidence that you can survive the next challenge too.

8 The person who has never failed lacks these essential qualities. They may appear successful on the surface, but they remain weak, unprepared for the inevitable difficulties that life brings to every journey.

9 Their first significant setback often devastates them because they have no experience with recovery, no familiarity with the process of getting back up.

4 Learn to distinguish between different types of failure, for not all setbacks carry the same lessons or require the same responses.

2 There are failures of effort—times when you simply didn't try hard enough, didn't persist long enough, didn't invest enough energy in achieving your goal.

3 These failures teach the value of commitment and the necessity of continued effort. They remind you that most worthwhile achievements require more work than initially expected.

4 There are failures of preparation—times when you attempted something without adequate knowledge, skills, or resources to succeed.

5 These failures teach the importance of learning before leaping, of developing competence before attempting performance, of building foundations before constructing buildings.

6 There are failures of judgment—times when you chose poorly, whether due to limited information, emotional pressure, or simply inexperience in making such decisions.

7 These failures teach discernment and the value of seeking counsel, of gathering more information before deciding, of considering long-term consequences rather than just immediate desires.

8 There are failures of timing—times when your actions were appropriate but your timing was wrong, when external circumstances made success impossible despite your best efforts.

9 These failures teach patience and the importance of reading situations carefully, of waiting for the right moment rather than forcing premature action.

10 And there are failures of impossibility—times when you attempted something that was never achievable given the constraints of reality, resources, or human limitation.

11 These failures teach acceptance and the wisdom of choosing goals that stretch you without breaking you, ambitions that challenge you without overwhelming you.

12 Each type of failure offers different gifts and requires different responses. The wise sojourner learns to diagnose which type of failure they have experienced so they can extract the appropriate lessons.

5 When failure arrives on your journey—and it will, for it visits every sojourner—resist the natural tendency to rush past it or deny its reality.

2 Give failure the attention it deserves, not as something to dwell on endlessly but as something to examine carefully for the wisdom it contains.

3 Ask yourself: What exactly went wrong? Was it your strategy, your execution, your timing, your preparation, or factors beyond your control?

4 Be honest in this examination without being harsh. The goal is learning, not self-punishment; understanding, not self-condemnation.

5 Ask also: What went right, even in this failure? For rarely is any attempt a complete disaster—usually some parts worked while others didn't.

6 These partial successes point toward what to keep as

you design your next attempt, just as the failures point toward what to change.

7 Consider what this failure reveals about your assumptions, your blind spots, your areas for growth. Often our greatest learning comes not from our successes, which confirm what we already know, but from our failures, which expose what we don't know.

8 Look for patterns across multiple failures. If you consistently struggle in certain areas, this points toward skills you need to develop, habits you need to change, or help you need to seek.

9 Remember that the pain of failure, while real and sometimes intense, is temporary. The lessons from failure, when properly extracted and applied, last a lifetime.

10 Do not rush to try again before you have understood why you failed the first time. Hasty repetition often leads to repeated failure, while careful analysis leads to improved performance.

6 One of failure's greatest gifts to the sojourner is its power to redirect your journey toward paths better suited to your gifts and calling.

2 Many people discover their true vocation only after failing at pursuits that seemed promising but proved wrong for them.

3 The failed engineer who becomes a successful teacher, the unsuccessful lawyer who finds fulfillment as a counselor, the defeated politician who thrives as a community organizer —all found their authentic path through the redirection that failure provided.

4 What feels like dead ends often turn out to be course corrections, steering you away from wrong destinations toward right ones.

5 Sometimes failure closes doors that needed to be closed,

eliminating options that would have led to greater unhappiness later.

6 The relationship that ends teaches you what you really need in partnership. The job you lose frees you to find work more aligned with your values. The business that fails teaches you lessons essential for the next venture.

7 Trust that failure's redirection, while often painful in the moment, may be protecting you from greater pain down the road or guiding you toward greater joy than you could have imagined.

8 Do not grieve too long over the paths that failure has closed to you. Instead, look at the new paths it has opened, the opportunities that become visible only when certain expectations are removed.

9 Many of life's greatest successes are built on the fertilizer of earlier failures, drawing strength from the decay of what didn't work to grow something that does.

10 The wise sojourner learns to see failure not as the end of their story but as the beginning of a new chapter, not as proof that they were on the wrong journey but as guidance toward the right direction.

7 Learning from failure requires developing the discipline to respond rather than react when setbacks occur.

2 The reactive response to failure is immediate and emotional—shame, anger, blame, despair, or the desperate urge to try the same thing again immediately.

3 These reactions are natural and human, but they rarely lead to the growth that failure offers. They keep you stuck in the pain of what went wrong rather than moving toward the learning that can make things go right.

4 The preferred approach to failure involves pausing, breathing, and creating space between the event and your next action.

5 In this space, you can process the emotions that failure brings without being controlled by them, examine what happened without being overwhelmed by it, and plan your next steps without being driven by desperation.

6 This response allows you to mine failure for its treasures while reaction leaves you buried under its debris.

7 Practice seeing failure as feedback rather than verdict, as information rather than condemnation, as redirection rather than rejection.

8 The sojourner who masters this perspective becomes antifragile—not just resilient in the face of setbacks but actually strengthened by them, growing stronger through difficulty rather than merely surviving it.

9 They begin to seek appropriate challenges rather than avoiding all risk, understanding that the right kind of failure speeds growth while the wrong kind of success can lead to stagnation.

10 They learn to fail fast and fail cheap when testing new approaches, gathering information quickly and inexpensively rather than investing everything in untested strategies.

8 As you develop a healthier relationship with failure, you may need to examine the stories you tell yourself about what success and failure mean.

2 Many people carry definitions inherited from family or childhood experiences that make failure seem more catastrophic than it actually is.

3 Some learned early that love and approval were conditional on performance, making any failure feel like a threat to their worth and belonging.

4 Others absorbed messages that equate personal value with achievement, making setbacks feel like evidence of inadequacy as human beings.

5 Still others developed perfectionist tendencies that make

any mistake feel like complete failure, any flaw like weakness.

6 These stories about failure often create more suffering than the failure itself, turning temporary setbacks into permanent shame, single events into character indictments.

7 The wise sojourner learns to rewrite these stories, developing narratives about failure that help growth rather than hinder it.

8 They practice separating their identity from their performance, their worth from their achievements, their value from their temporary circumstances.

9 They learn to see failure as one of many experiences in a full life rather than the defining experience that determines everything else.

10 This rewriting takes time and practice, especially if the old stories have deep roots. Be patient with yourself as you develop new ways of thinking about setbacks and mistakes.

11 Seek out examples of people who have failed significantly and gone on to meaningful success, studying how they navigated their setbacks and what attitudes helped them recover.

12 Remember that the most inspiring stories often include significant failures that seemed devastating at the time but proved essential to the final success.

9 Consider how failure serves not just individual sojourners but the human community as a whole.

2 Every medical breakthrough came through countless failed experiments. Every technological advance built on thousands of attempts that didn't work. Every social improvement grew from movements that faced repeated setbacks.

3 The vaccines that save lives today exist because researchers failed repeatedly until they found formulations that worked. The devices that connect the world were built by

inventors whose early prototypes crashed, exploded, or simply sat silent.

4 Even this moment, as you read these words, you benefit from the accumulated failures of countless people who tried and failed and tried again until they succeeded.

5 Your own failures contribute to this great human project of learning through trial and error, of advancing through setbacks, of succeeding through continued effort despite repeated disappointment.

6 When you fail at something and then share what you learned, you save others from making the same mistakes. When you document what doesn't work, you help others find what does.

7 Your willingness to risk failure encourages others to take their own necessary risks.

8 Your resilience in the face of setbacks models possibility for those facing their own difficulties.

9 In this way, even your failures serve purposes larger than your individual journey, contributing to the collective wisdom of the human community.

10 Do not underestimate the value of this contribution or feel that your setbacks are merely personal problems. They are part of the larger human story of growth through adversity.

10

As your journey continues and you gain experience with both failure and recovery, you may find that your relationship with risk itself begins to change.

2 Instead of avoiding all possibility of failure, you begin to seek the right kinds of challenges—difficult enough to stretch you but not so overwhelming as to crush you.

3 You learn to distinguish between reckless risks that serve no good purpose and courageous risks that serve your growth or the benefit of others.

4 You develop the wisdom to know when to persist

through difficulty and when to recognize that persistence would be futile, when to adapt your approach and when to change your destination entirely.

5 Most importantly, you discover that the fear of failure had been holding you back from attempts that might have succeeded, from experiences that would have enriched your journey regardless of their outcome.

6 The person who has learned to fail well often discovers they were capable of far more than they had imagined, not because failure made them stronger but because overcoming the fear of failure allowed their strength to emerge.

7 They find themselves taking creative risks, building meaningful relationships, pursuing important goals, and contributing to causes larger than themselves—all because they no longer need to guarantee success before they begin.

8 This freedom from perfectionism opens possibilities that were hidden when avoiding failure was the primary goal.

9 It allows for experimentation, innovation, and growth that can only happen when you're willing to look foolish, to make mistakes, to fail.

11 There will be times on your journey when failure feels too heavy to bear, when setbacks pile up like storms that never end, when the lessons feel less important than the pain.

2 In these moments, remember that you are not the first sojourner to face such difficulties, nor will you be the last.

3 Others have walked through valleys deeper than yours and emerged into sunlight again. Others have faced failures that seemed to shatter everything they had built and found ways to build again.

4 Their stories remind you that the human ability for recovery far exceeds what seems possible in moments of despair.

5 Seek out these stories, whether from books, from mentors, or from conversations with those who have traveled similar paths.

6 Allow yourself to be encouraged by proof that resilience is not rare but common, that recovery is not exceptional but normal for those who persist.

7 Remember too that the darkest failures often come before the brightest successes, not because life is dramatic but because failure often clears away everything that was preventing success.

8 The business failure that forces you to examine your priorities, the relationship failure that teaches you to love more wisely, the health failure that shows you what truly matters—these may be preparing you for achievements that you could never have imagined before.

9 Trust the process even when you cannot see the ending, especially when the current failure feels like the end of your story rather than a difficult chapter within it.

12 As you master the art of learning from failure, you become a gift to other sojourners who face their own setbacks and struggles.

2 Your presence reminds them that failure is survivable, that setbacks are temporary, that mistakes are correctable.

3 Your example shows them that it is possible to face disappointment with grace, to gain wisdom from difficulty, to grow stronger through troubles.

4 When you speak honestly about your own failures and what you learned from them, you give others permission to be honest about theirs.

5 When you demonstrate strength without pretending that recovery was easy, you offer hope without minimizing the struggle.

6 When you show that your failures guided you toward

better paths, you help others trust that their setbacks might do the same.

7 In this way, your relationship with failure becomes part of your contribution to the human journey, part of how you serve the community of sojourners.

8 You become someone who helps others fail better—not by helping them avoid all mistakes, but by helping them recover more quickly and learn when mistakes occur.

9 This may be one of the most valuable gifts you can offer: the modeling of a healthy relationship with failure that allows for both high standards and self-compassion.

10 For in the end, the sojourner's journey is not about avoiding failure but about failing forward, not about never falling but about

always getting back up, not about perfection but about progress through the accumulation of wisdom gained from both success and setback.

11 May your failures serve your growth, may your setbacks redirect you toward better paths, and may your recovery from disappointment inspire others to persist through their own difficulties.

12 For this is the way of the wise sojourner: to learn from everything, to grow through troubles, and to trust that even failure serves the larger purpose of becoming who you were meant to be.

19

the Book of Celebration

1 Consider how the sojourner moves through this world, often so focused on reaching the next destination that they miss the beauty of the present moment, so concerned with future security that they forget to notice today's blessings.

2 Many people live as though joy were a luxury they cannot afford, as though gratitude were a weakness that leaves them vulnerable, as though celebration is a distraction from serious pursuits.

3 They postpone happiness until conditions are perfect, delay gratitude until all problems are solved, put away celebration until some distant achievement makes it seem deserved.

4 "I will be happy when I get the promotion, when I find

the right relationship, when I have enough money, when my health improves, when my children succeed." Thus, they spend their entire journey waiting for permission to be happy.

5 Others swing to the opposite extreme, pursuing pleasure with desperate intensity, confusing celebration with escapism, mistaking entertainment for joy, substituting artificial highs for authentic happiness.

6 But there is a wiser way to move through this brief journey—with hearts open to wonder, eyes trained to notice goodness, and spirits ready to celebrate the gifts that appear along the path.

7 For the sojourner who understands the temporary nature of this journey knows that joy deferred is often joy denied, that gratitude withheld loses its power to transform, that celebrations postponed may never come.

8 The awareness of life's brevity does not diminish the call to celebrate—it intensifies it, making each moment of genuine joy more precious, each reason for gratitude more significant.

2 Celebration is not the reward for a journey completed but the fuel that sustains sojourners along the way.

2 Like rest that restores energy for the next day, like food that nourishes the body, celebration restores the spirit for whatever challenges lie ahead.

3 The sojourner who never celebrates grows weary not just in body but in soul, losing the sense of wonder that makes the journey meaningful, forgetting why the destination matters in the first place.

4 Joy is not unimportant but essential—as necessary for human growth as water for a garden, as vital for the spirit as oxygen for the lungs.

5 When you celebrate, you do more than mark an achievement or acknowledge a blessing. You remind yourself

that life contains goodness worth recognizing, that the journey includes moments of light within the shadows.

6 Celebration trains your attention to notice what is going well rather than only what is going wrong, to see abundance rather than only short supply, to recognize progress rather than only problems.

7 This shift in attention does not deny reality's difficulties but places them in proper perspective, understanding that both light and shadow are part of every journey.

8 The person who develops the discipline of celebration discovers that joy is not dependent on circumstances being perfect but on awareness being present.

9 They learn to find reasons for gratitude even in flawed situations, sources of wonder even in ordinary moments, cause for celebration even in simple experiences.

10 This is not rose-colored-glasses or denial of real problems, but the recognition that life contains both suffering and blessing, both challenge and gift.

3 The art of celebration begins with learning to savor—to slow down enough to truly taste your food, to pause long enough to really see a sunset, to be still enough to feel the warmth of connection with another person.

2 Savoring requires presence, the willingness to be fully where you are rather than rushing toward where you think you should be going.

3 In a culture that values speed, efficiency, and constant productivity, savoring feels like a luxury you cannot afford. But for the sojourner who knows time is limited, savoring becomes essential wisdom.

4 When you savor, you extract the full nourishment from each experience rather than consuming life like fast food—quickly and without really tasting.

5 Savor the morning coffee as if you had never tasted

anything like it before. Notice its warmth, its aroma, the way it awakens your senses and prepares you for the day ahead.

6 Savor conversations with people you love as if you might not have unlimited opportunities to hear their voice, share their thoughts, witness their laughter.

7 Savor moments of beauty—the way light falls across a room, the sound of rain on the roof, the feeling of a cool breeze on a warm day—as if you were storing up for times when beauty seems scarce.

8 Savor your own achievements, not with arrogance but with honest appreciation for the effort invested, the skills developed, the obstacles overcome.

9 The practice of savoring transforms ordinary experiences into celebrations, routine moments into reasons for gratitude, simple pleasures into profound gifts.

4 Gratitude is not merely a feeling but a discipline—a conscious choice to notice and acknowledge the good that exists in your life, regardless of what may be missing or difficult.

2 This discipline becomes especially important during challenging times of the journey, when problems dominate your attention and blessings fade into the background of your thoughts.

3 When illness strikes, practice gratitude for the parts of your body that still function well. When relationships struggle, appreciate the connections that remain strong. When work becomes difficult, acknowledge the abilities that enable you to contribute.

4 This is not denial of real problems or pretending that everything is fine when it is not. This is the recognition that even in difficult circumstances, some things remain worth celebrating.

5 The practice of gratitude during hardship requires

effort, like physical exercise when you do not feel like moving. But like exercise, it creates strength that serves you well when easier times return.

6 Develop the habit of noticing three specific things you are grateful for each day—not because three is a magic number, but because the discipline of looking for specific goodness trains your attention to notice what you might otherwise take for granted.

7 Express gratitude not just in private reflection but in public acknowledgment. Tell people when they have contributed to your life. Write notes of appreciation. Speak words of thanks for kindness received.

8 This expression of gratitude creates a cycle of goodness—your recognition encourages others to continue positive behavior, their continued kindness gives you more to appreciate, your appreciation makes you more aware of goodness everywhere.

9 The person who practices gratitude during difficult times discovers that this discipline does not eliminate problems but it does prevent problems from eliminating joy.

5 Meaningful celebration requires rituals and traditions that mark significant moments in the journey and create shared memory with fellow sojourners.

2 Rituals are not empty ceremonies but powerful tools that help you pay attention to what matters, remember what you might forget, and connect current experiences to the larger patterns of meaning.

3 Some rituals you inherit from those who traveled before you—holidays that connect you to history, ceremonies that mark life's transitions, traditions that tie families and communities together across generations.

4 Receive these inherited rituals with gratitude while adapting them to fit your current understanding and

circumstances. Honor the wisdom of those who came before while making celebrations meaningful for yourself.

5 Other rituals you must create yourself—new traditions that create markers unique to your journey, celebrations that acknowledge achievements no one else may recognize as important.

6 Create rituals around first days and last days, around beginnings and endings, around ordinary moments that feel extraordinary in your life.

7 Celebrate the anniversary of recovery from illness, the completion of difficult projects, the anniversaries of meaningful relationships, the day you moved to a new place, the moment you decided to change direction.

8 The ritual need not be fancy—sharing a special meal, visiting a meaningful place, gathering with people who matter to you.

9 What makes a ritual powerful is not its elaborateness but its purpose, not its cost but its meaning, not its appearance to others but its meaning to you.

10 Through ritual and tradition, you create markers along your journey that help you remember how far you have traveled, what you have learned, whom you have become.

6 Celebration becomes most powerful when shared with fellow sojourners, transforming individual joy into a community blessing, personal achievement into community treasure.

2 When you celebrate alone, you experience the satisfaction of recognition. When you celebrate with others, you multiply the joy through connection and create shared memories that enrich all.

3 But choosing whom to celebrate with requires wisdom. Not everyone can genuinely rejoice in your good fortune. Not everyone has the capacity to appreciate what brings you joy.

4 Seek out those who can celebrate your successes without feeling minmized by them, who can share your happiness without needing to redirect attention to their own needs.

5 Avoid those who minimize your achievements, who turn your celebrations into competitions, who use your joy as an opportunity to share their own problems.

6 The ability to genuinely celebrate with others is a mark of maturity and spiritual health. Those who possess it make worthy companions for the journey.

7 Learn also to be the kind of person others want to celebrate with—someone who can rejoice in others' good fortune without jealousy, who can appreciate achievements in fields different from your own, who can find genuine happiness in seeing fellow sojourners succeed.

8 This capacity for shared celebration creates bonds stronger than mere shared struggle, relationships based on mutual appreciation rather than only mutual need.

9 When you master the art of celebrating with others, you discover that joy shared is joy multiplied, that good news welcomed enthusiastically returns to you in unexpected ways.

7 Learn to celebrate progress as well as completion, improvement as well as perfection, effort as well as achievement.

2 The journey toward any meaningful goal is long, with many steps between the beginning and ending. If you wait until final completion to celebrate, you may wait so long that momentum dies and motivation fades.

3 Celebrate the first page written as well as the finished book, the first mile run as well as the completed marathon, the first conversation as well as the relationship.

4 Celebrate learning as much as knowing, growing as much as arriving, becoming as much as being.

5 This practice of celebrating progress sustains energy for long-term efforts and helps you appreciate the journey rather than only the destination.

6 It also teaches humility—recognizing that all achievement is built from small steps, that all mastery develops from repeated practice, that all success emerges from accumulated effort.

7 The person who can only celebrate perfection rarely celebrates at all. The person who can celebrate progress finds reasons for joy in every season of growth.

8 Mark the milestones of your learning—the first time you understood a difficult concept, the day you finally mastered a challenging skill, the moment you realized you had changed in ways you had been seeking to change.

9 These internal victories often go unnoticed by others but they represent the real substance of personal growth and deserve recognition as much as any external achievement.

8 The discipline of celebration includes learning when not to celebrate, recognizing that timing and appropriateness matter in the art of marking meaningful moments.

2 There is a time for celebration and a time for solemnness, a time for joy and a time for mourning, a time for festivity and a time for reflection.

3 Premature celebration can cheapen achievement that has not yet been fully earned. Inappropriate celebration can seem insensitive to others who are struggling. Forced celebration can feel hollow when authentic joy is not present.

4 Develop the wisdom to read the season—both your own and the season of those around you. Sometimes the most loving response is to postpone celebration until a more appropriate time.

5 Sometimes the most honest response is to acknowledge

that while others are celebrating, you are not yet ready to join them. This is not failure but self-awareness.

6 The absence of celebratory feeling does not always mean absence of progress or success. Sometimes achievement comes wrapped in exhaustion, relief, or quiet satisfaction rather than outward joy.

7 Learn to recognize and honor these quieter forms of celebration—the deep contentment of work well done, the peaceful satisfaction of a goal reached, the gentle gratitude for a challenge overcome.

8 Not every victory requires a party. Not every achievement calls for public recognition. Not every milestone needs a dramatic marking.

9 Sometimes the most appropriate celebration is a moment of silent gratitude, a private acknowledgment of growth, a quiet recognition of grace received.

9 As your journey progresses, celebration becomes not just something you do but part of who you are—a person who notices goodness, acknowledges blessing, and finds reasons for gratitude even in ordinary circumstances.

2 This transformation changes how you move through the world. Instead of scanning constantly for problems to solve or threats to avoid, you also notice beauty to appreciate and kindness to acknowledge.

3 This shift in attention does not make you naive about real difficulties or blind to genuine problems. But it does create a more balanced perspective that includes both shadow and light in your field of vision.

4 People will notice this change in you. They will be drawn to your ability to find joy in simple things, your capacity to appreciate what others take for granted, your skill at creating meaningful moments from ordinary experiences.

5 Your example gives others permission to celebrate their

own lives, to find their own reasons for gratitude, to create their own meaningful rituals and traditions.

6 In this way, your discipline of celebration becomes a gift not only to yourself but to everyone whose life intersects with yours on the journey.

7 You become someone who adds lightness to heavy moments, who notices achievements others might miss, who remembers to mark milestones that might otherwise pass unnoticed.

8 This is a form of leadership—leading by example in the art of living fully, in the practice of gratitude, in the discipline of joy.

10
The ultimate celebration for the sojourner is the celebration of the journey itself—not just its highlights and achievements, but the whole experience of being human for this brief time.

2 When you truly understand that your time here is limited, every moment becomes worthy of some form of appreciation—not because every moment is pleasant, but because every moment is yours to experience.

3 Celebrate your ability to feel, even when the feelings are difficult. Celebrate your ability to think, even when thoughts are confusing. Celebrate your power to choose, even when choices are hard.

4 Celebrate the miraculous fact of your existence—that against all odds, you are here, conscious, capable of love and learning, able to contribute something unique to the world's story.

5 Celebrate the companions you have found along the way—the friends who have enriched your journey, the teachers who have expanded your understanding, the strangers who have shown unexpected kindness.

6 Celebrate the challenges that have strengthened you, the

failures that have taught you, the losses that have deepened your appreciation for what remains.

7 Celebrate the beauty you have witnessed—sunsets that took your breath away, music that moved your soul, acts of courage that inspired your spirit.

8 Celebrate the love you have given and received—imperfect perhaps, limited certainly, but real and meaningful in ways that echo beyond your understanding.

9 This celebration of the journey—with all its mixed experiences and varied outcomes—represents the gratitude of someone who has learned to say yes to life as it actually is rather than only as they wished it might be.

10 In the end, the greatest celebration is the simple recognition: "I was here. I experienced this extraordinary gift of consciousness. I participated in the mystery of being human. I added my unique note to the great song that has been playing since the beginning of time."

11 This is enough. This is more than enough. This is cause for the deepest gratitude and the most profound celebration—not because the journey was perfect, but because it was yours.

12 Let your life be a celebration of the gift you have been given, and let your celebration be a gift to all who travel alongside you.

20

the Book of Legacy

1 Consider this truth that confronts every sojourner on the journey: though you cannot remain in this world forever, something of you can and will endure beyond your departure.

2 Every person who walks this earth leaves traces—some visible, some invisible, some intentional, some accidental. The question is not whether you will leave a legacy, but what kind of legacy you will leave.

3 For legacy is not reserved for the famous, the wealthy, or the powerful. Every conversation shapes someone's thinking, every kindness plants a seed, every example teaches a lesson, every choice creates a ripple that moves outward in ways you may never see.

4 The mother who teaches her child to share creates a legacy of generosity that may flow through generations. The teacher who believes in a struggling student creates a legacy of possibility that may change multiple lives. The neighbor who shows up in times of need creates a legacy of community that strengthens the whole.

5 Yet many sojourners give little thought to what they are creating through their daily choices, unaware that they are constantly writing the story that others will remember and repeat.

6 They focus on what they can get from this world rather than what they can give to it, on what they can accumulate rather than what they can contribute, on temporary gains rather than lasting gifts.

7 But the wise sojourner understands that since they cannot take anything with them when they go, the only true treasures are those they leave behind—and the most valuable of these are not material possessions but the ways they have shaped hearts, minds, and souls.

2 Legacy lives first in the ordinary moments that seem insignificant at the time but prove important in retrospect.

2 It is the father who listens carefully when his child speaks, teaching through attention the lesson that every person's voice matters.

3 It is the coworker who takes time to help someone learn a skill, planting seeds of competence and confidence that may bloom years later.

4 It is the friend who offers comfort in grief, demonstrating that suffering need not be faced alone, that friendship can carry what individuals cannot bear.

5 These moments require no special platform, no public recognition, no extraordinary resources—only the recognition that every interaction is an opportunity to add light or darkness to someone's journey.

6 The ripples from such moments travel far beyond what you can see. The child who feels truly heard may grow up to listen carefully to their own children. The person who receives help may become someone who helps others. The one who finds comfort in grief may become a comforter to others who mourn.

7 What seems like a single kind word, a moment of patience, may become the turning point in someone's story, the memory they return to for strength, the example they follow when facing their own choices.

8 Therefore, approach each day with the understanding that you are constantly creating legacy through the accumulation of ordinary moments lived with intention and care.

9 The legacy of the ordinary is often the most profound because it touches the daily experience of being human, shaping not spectacular achievements but the quality of everyday life.

3 Beyond the ripples of daily kindness, legacy takes shape through the conscious act of passing on what you have learned to those who come after you.

2 This is the sacred responsibility of every generation: to serve as a bridge between the wisdom of those who came before and the needs of those who will follow.

3 You have inherited knowledge, skills, values, and insights from countless others who invested in your growth. What will you do with this inheritance?

4 The teacher who not only imparts information but demonstrates how to think, how to question, how to wonder, leaves a legacy that outlasts any particular lesson.

5 The craftsperson who trains an apprentice passes on not just technical skill but the pride of doing work well, the satisfaction of creating something useful, the dignity of honest labor.

6 The parent who shares not just rules but the reasoning behind them, not just expectations but the love that motivates them, creates a legacy of wisdom rather than mere obedience.

7 The mentor who invests in someone's potential creates a legacy of belief—the profound gift of being seen and valued before you fully see and value yourself.

8 Such investment requires patience, for you may never see the full fruit of what you plant. The student may not appreciate the lesson until years later. The apprentice may not understand the gift until they become a journeyman. The child may not grasp love until they become a parent.

9 But this is the nature of legacy—it operates on a timeline longer than individual life, creating value that grows across generations.

10 When you teach someone to fish, you feed them for a lifetime. When you teach them to teach others to fish, you create a legacy that feeds many lifetimes.

4 Legacy also lives in the traditions you create and the ones you choose to continue or change.

2 Some traditions you inherit from family, community, or culture—patterns of celebration, methods of marking important moments, ways of treating others, approaches to work and rest.

3 With each tradition, you face a choice: Will you pass it on unchanged, modify it to better serve current needs, or allow it to end with you?

4 The wise sojourner evaluates inherited traditions not with automatic acceptance or rejection, but with discernment: Does this tradition serve love? Does it build community? Does it add meaning to life? Does it honor what is best in human nature?

5 Those traditions that serve these purposes deserve to be preserved and passed on. Those that divide, diminish, or harm may need to be transformed or allowed to die.

6 But legacy is not only about continuing what was given to you—it is also about creating new traditions that serve the unique needs of your time and place.

7 The family that establishes a weekly ritual of sharing what they're grateful for creates a legacy of appreciation. The community that begins a tradition of caring for its elderly creates a legacy of honor. The workplace that develops customs of celebrating both successes and learning from failures creates a legacy of resilience.

8 These new traditions may seem small when they begin, but they can become the foundations on which future generations build their own sense of meaning and belonging.

9 You are always both heir and ancestor, receiver and giver, student and teacher. What you do with what you've inherited shapes what you pass on.

10 Consider carefully: What traditions from your past deserve to continue? What new traditions does your time need? How can you be a bridge that honors the past while serving the future?

5 The deepest form of legacy lies not in what you say or even what you do, but in who you become and how that shapes others simply through your presence.

2 Character creates legacy through influence that operates beneath the level of conscious instruction—the way your integrity inspires others to be honest, your courage gives others permission to be brave, your compassion teaches others to care.

3 People learn more from watching how you handle difficulty than from hearing your theories about resilience. They absorb more about love from observing how you treat those who can do nothing for you than from listening to your speeches about kindness.

4 The legacy of character operates through modeling rather than preaching, through demonstration rather than talk.

5 Children learn how to be human not primarily from what their parents tell them but from what they witness in their parents' daily choices, reactions, and relationships.

6 Colleagues learn about leadership not from management seminars but from observing how their supervisors treat people when things go wrong, how they share credit and accept blame, how they balance competing demands.

7 Friends learn about loyalty, honesty, and love not from philosophical discussions but from experiencing these qualities in relationship with you over time.

8 This kind of legacy requires the longest investment because character develops slowly, through countless small choices made consistently over years.

9 But it creates the most enduring influence because it shapes not just what people know but who they become.

10 The person who consistently chooses integrity over advantage, kindness over convenience, truth over comfort, creates a legacy that echoes in the choices of everyone who witnessed these priorities in action

6 As you consider the legacy you are creating, remember that its value lies not in its size or visibility but in its alignment with what matters most.

2 The world often measures legacy by monuments built, wealth accumulated, or recognition received. But these external markers may have little connection to the true influence a life creates.

3 The unknown teacher whose students become compassionate leaders leaves a greater legacy than the famous person whose influence encourages selfishness.

4 The parent who raises children with strong values leaves

a greater legacy than the executive who builds a successful company through exploitation.

5 The friend who provides steady love and support through decades leaves a greater legacy than the celebrity who inspires temporary admiration.

6 Legacy is measured not by how many people know your name but by how many people are better because they knew you.

7 Not by what you achieved for yourself but by what you made possible for others.

8 Not by how much you accumulated but by how much you contributed.

9 Not by how long you are remembered but by how lovingly you are remembered by those whose lives you touched directly.

10 The most beautiful legacies are often the most invisible —threads of kindness, wisdom, and love woven so naturally into the fabric of daily life that they become indistinguishable from the pattern itself.

7 To create the legacy you truly want requires living with what some call "legacy consciousness"—awareness that your current choices are shaping the story that will outlast you.

2 This consciousness brings both weight and freedom to decision-making. Weight, because you recognize that your choices matter beyond their immediate consequences. Freedom, because you can choose what story you want to write.

3 When facing a difficult decision, ask yourself: "How do I want this choice to read in the story of my life? What would I want people to learn from how I handle this situation? What example am I setting for those who look to me?"

4 This does not mean living for others' approval or trying to create a perfect image. It means living with integrity that aligns your daily choices with your deepest values.

5 Legacy consciousness also means recognizing that you are always teaching—whether or not you intend to be, whether or not anyone seems to be paying attention.

6 Your children are learning how to handle anger by watching how you handle anger. Your colleagues are learning about teamwork by observing how you work with others. Your friends are learning about loyalty by experiencing your friendship.

7 You cannot not teach. You cannot not influence. You cannot not leave marks on the lives around you. The only choice is what kind of marks you leave.

8 Living with legacy consciousness means taking responsibility for the influence you have, using it intentionally to add light rather than darkness to the world.

9 It means asking regularly: "What am I teaching through my example? What am I creating through my choices? What seeds am I planting through my words and actions?"

8 The ultimate gift of legacy thinking is that it transforms how you understand your own mortality.

2 When you recognize that something of you can endure beyond your physical presence, death becomes not the end of your story but the beginning of its next chapter.

3 The love you have shown continues to flow through hearts you have touched. The wisdom you have shared continues to guide decisions you will never see. The kindness you have practiced continues to inspire actions you will never know about.

4 This is how your absence can be felt as presence—not through supernatural intervention, but through the natural continuation of influence you set in motion while you were here.

5 The parent who loved well lives on in the security their children feel and the love those children give to their own families.

6 The teacher who inspired learning lives on in the curiosity their students maintain and the questions those students teach others to ask.

7 The friend who offered faithful support lives on in the confidence their friendship built and the support that confidence enables them to offer others.

8 In this way, legacy becomes a form of immortality available to every person—not the preservation of the self, but the continuation of the self's best contributions.

9 You cannot take your possessions with you when you go, but you can leave your influence behind to continue working in the world.

10 You cannot extend your own life indefinitely, but you can invest it in ways that extend its impact indefinitely.

9 As your time as a sojourner draws toward its eventual end, legacy consciousness brings both urgency and peace.

2 Urgency, because you recognize that time to create and contribute is limited. Every day matters. Every interaction is an opportunity. Every choice shapes the story.

3 Peace, because you know that a life lived with intention and love creates value that transcends the life itself. What you have given will continue giving. Who you have been will continue influencing. How you have loved will continue healing.

4 The person approaching the end of their journey with this understanding can face departure with sadness at leaving but satisfaction in having used their time meaningfully.

5 They have loved well, served faithfully, contributed generously. They have passed on what they received and added their own unique gifts to the human story.

6 Their legacy is not a monument to themselves but a gift to the future—seeds planted in soil they will not see bloom, light kindled in darkness they will not see illuminated.

7 This is perhaps the most profound aspect of legacy: it is inherently selfless. You create it not for your own benefit but for the benefit of those who will continue the journey after you.

8 In giving this gift, you join the great company of all who have used their brief time here to serve the long purposes of love, wisdom, and human growth.

10 The beauty of legacy is that it is available to everyone, requires no special qualifications, and can begin at any moment.

2 You need not be wealthy to leave wealth—the wealth of love, wisdom, and kindness that enriches every life it touches.

3 You need not be famous to be influential—the influence you have on those closest to you may prove more significant than any public recognition.

4 You need not have perfect circumstances to create perfect gifts—some of the best legacies have emerged from the most challenging situations.

5 You need not wait until you are old to begin creating legacy—every stage of life offers opportunities to give, teach, and influence.

6 The teenager who befriends the lonely creates legacy. The young adult who chooses integrity over advantage creates legacy. The parent who listens more than lectures creates legacy. The elder who shares wisdom rather than complaints creates legacy.

7 Begin where you are, with what you have, for those within your reach. Legacy is not created through grand gestures but through faithful stewardship of ordinary opportunities.

8 Choose to see each day as a chance to add to the story you are writing with your life, each interaction as an opportunity to plant seeds that may grow long after you are gone.

9 Live as if your choices matter beyond your own experience—because they do. Love as if your love could heal wounds you may never see—because it can. Give as if your gifts could transform futures you will never witness—because they will.

10 For in the end, legacy is love expressed through time, wisdom shared across generations, goodness multiplied through influence—the eternal gift that finite beings can give to the infinite story of human growth.

11 This is your opportunity and your responsibility as a sojourner: to use your brief time here to create lasting good, to let your temporary presence create permanent gifts, to ensure that your absence will be felt as presence in the lives you have touched.

12 May you create a legacy worthy of the love that created you, worthy of the time that was given to you, worthy of the trust that others have placed in you, and worthy of the future that depends on what you choose to leave behind.

21

the Book of Yesterday

1 Consider how we relate to the past as we journey through this life, how memories follow us like shadows.

2 Many people carry their past like a heavy burden, allowing yesterday's pain to poison today's possibilities. They look backward with either rose-colored glasses that make everything seem better than it was, or through dark lenses that make every memory a source of regret.

3 Some flee from their past as if it were a pursuing enemy, spending their energy running from what has already happened rather than walking in the present moment. Others become trapped within it, living as prisoners in cells built from old hurts and faded dreams.

4 Still others use the past as an escape from present

responsibilities, retreating into selective memories of "better times" whenever current reality becomes challenging or uncomfortable.

5 But there is a wiser way to relate to what has been—not as burden or prison, not as enemy or refuge, but as a reservoir of experience from which to draw wisdom, strength, and understanding for the journey ahead.

6 The past is neither to be worshipped nor cursed, neither to be erased nor allowed to dominate.

7 It is to be understood, learned from, and integrated into the fullness of who we are becoming.

8 For what has happened cannot be changed, but its influence over us can be transformed.

9 Past events are fixed, but their meaning in our lives can be rewritten.

10 This transformation requires courage to face what was, wisdom to see it clearly, and grace to release what no longer serves while keeping what can help.

2 Understand this truth: the past is not an excuse for present failure or future limitations, but it is a reason that must be navigated, negotiated, and redirected in its impact upon us.

2 Those who use the past as excuse say, "I cannot succeed because of what was done to me," or "I am broken because of what happened then." In doing so, they surrender their power to the unchangeable and remain victims of time itself.

3 But those who see the past as reason say, "I understand why I struggle because of what I experienced, and therefore I can work with these patterns, healing what needs healing and strengthening what has been weakened."

4 The difference is not in denial of the past's impact, but in claiming responsibility for the present response.

5 We cannot choose what happened to us, but we can choose what we do with what happened to us.

6 To succumb completely to the impacts of the past is to live in the past, trapped like a caged animal with all its anxieties and fears, dreaming of a future yet afraid to step into the present moment.

7 Those who live in the past feel the walls of yesterday closing in around them each day.

8 They seek distractions to numb the symptoms of yesterday's pain—endless entertainment, substances, busyness, or fantasy—anything to avoid facing what needs to be faced.

9 To such people, the past becomes a cesspool of pain, regret, and unnecessary weight.

10 Layer upon layer of distorted memories pile up, each viewed through faulty lenses that pull them further into the mire rather than offering wisdom for the journey.

11 They see only failure where there was also learning, only pain where there was also growth, only endings where there were also beginnings.

12 Their vision becomes clouded by the dust of old grievances and the fog of persistent regret.

13 But the past need not be a cesspool. It can become a reservoir—a source of knowledge and experience to draw upon as we navigate present challenges and future opportunities.

3 How then shall we transform our relationship with what has been? How do we convert what could be weakness into strength, what could be bondage into wisdom?

2 First, face the past with honest eyes. Do not minimize what was difficult, nor exaggerate what was painful.

3 See events as they were, not as you wished they had been, nor as your fears have made them seem.

4 Many memories are like photographs that have been exposed to too much light—the details have become washed out, leaving only impressions that may not match

the original reality. Time and emotion can distort what actually happened.

5 Second, recognize that your responses to past events were made with the information, maturity, and resources you had at that time.

6 You cannot judge your yesterday-self by today's standards of knowledge and wisdom.

7 The child who did not speak up against abuse lacked the strength and understanding that the adult now possesses.

8 The young person who made poor choices was working with limited experience and immature judgment.

9 The person who trusted the wrong people, who missed important signs, who failed to protect themselves or others—they were doing the best they could with what they knew and what they were capable of in that moment.

10 This does not excuse harmful actions taken against others, but it releases the excessive self-blame that keeps many people trapped in cycles of guilt and shame.

11 Third, separate what happened from what you made it mean.

12 Events are facts; meanings are interpretations.

13 The same event can carry different meanings depending on the lens through which it is viewed.

14 A failure in business can mean "I am incompetent" or "I learned valuable lessons about what doesn't work." A betrayal by a friend can mean "I cannot trust anyone" or "I can learn to choose relationships more wisely."

15 The events remain the same, but their power over your present and future changes dramatically when you change the meaning you assign to them.

4 To remove the negative emotions attached to past events requires both time and intentional work.

2 These emotions—anger, fear, shame, resentment—are

like barnacles attached to the hull of a ship, creating drag that slows forward movement.

3 Begin by acknowledging these emotions without judgment. They arose for reasons, often as protection against further harm.

4 Anger defended against vulnerability. Fear warned of similar dangers. Shame attempted to prevent rejection by others.

5 But what once served as protection can become a prison.

6 The anger that once motivated you to escape a harmful situation can become a consuming fire that burns your present relationships. The fear that once kept you safe can become a wall that keeps out all possibilities.

7 Practice observing these emotions as visitors rather than permanent residents.

8 When anger arises from a past hurt, notice it: "Anger about that old situation is visiting me now." When shame from a past mistake surfaces, acknowledge it: "Shame from that time is here again."

9 This perspective creates space between you and the emotion. You are not your anger; you are the one who sometimes experiences anger. You are not your shame; you are the one who sometimes feels shame.

10 Then practice responding to these emotional visitors with compassion rather than resistance. Fighting against them often strengthens them. Instead, you might say, "I understand why you're here, old pain. You're trying to protect me. But I'm safe now, and I can handle things differently."

11 Seek to understand the story these emotions are telling you. What were they trying to protect? What need were they attempting to meet? Often beneath anger is hurt, beneath fear is the desire for safety, beneath shame is the longing for acceptance.

12 As you understand the deeper needs, you can find healthier ways to meet them in the present rather than being driven by the strategies that formed in the past.

5 Remember that healing is not forgetting.

2 You need not erase your memories to be free from their negative control. Indeed, trying to forget often gives memories more power, not less.

3 Healing is the transformation of relationship—moving from being controlled by the past to being informed by it, from being wounded by memories to being strengthened by the wisdom they contain.

4 Consider how a broken bone, when properly set and healed, often becomes stronger at the break point than it was before. So too can the places where we have been wounded become sources of particular strength and compassion.

5 Those who have known betrayal can develop exceptional ability to recognize trustworthiness in others.

6 Those who have experienced loss can offer unique comfort to others in grief.

7 Those who have struggled with addiction can guide others toward recovery.

8 This transformation does not happen automatically. It requires the conscious choice to mine the lessons from painful experiences rather than simply enduring their ongoing effects.

9 Ask yourself: What did this experience teach me about human nature? About my own strengths and limitations? About what I value most? About how I want to treat others? About what brings meaning to life?

10 These questions shift focus from "Why did this happen to me?" to "How can I use what happened to live more wisely now?" The first question often leads to resentment and despair; the second leads to growth and purpose.

11 Practice gratitude for the strength you developed through surviving difficult times. This does not mean being grateful for the harm that was done, but recognizing the resilience, wisdom, and compassion that emerged from your response to that harm.

6 Understand that you are not responsible for everything that happened in your past, but you are responsible for what you do with it now. This is both the burden and the freedom of present-moment living.

2 Some carry false guilt for things beyond their control—the divorce of parents, the death of loved ones, the mental illness of family members, the choices made by others.

3 Children especially tend to blame themselves for adult problems they could neither cause nor solve.

4 Release yourself from responsibility for what was never yours to control. You could not have prevented every bad thing that happened. You could not have fixed every broken person in your life. You could not have known then what you know now.

5 At the same time, take full responsibility for your response moving forward.

6 You cannot change what was done to you, but you can change what you do with what was done to you.

7 This includes making amends where your past actions harmed others, seeking help for patterns that continue to cause problems, and choosing different responses when similar situations arise.

8 It also includes the responsibility to not pass on unchanged the harmful patterns you experienced. The cycle of hurt passing from generation to generation can stop with you.

9 Those who were criticized harshly as children can choose to speak encouragingly to the children in their lives. Those who were neglected can choose to be present and

attentive. Those who were controlled can choose to respect others' autonomy.

10 In this way, your healing becomes a gift not only to yourself but to all whose lives you touch.

11 Your transformation of the past's influence creates ripples of positive change that extend far beyond your own experience.

7 Learn to distinguish between remembering and reliving.

2 Remembering is recalling what happened with your current awareness and wisdom.

3 Reliving is being pulled back into the emotional state you were in when it happened.

4 When you remember, you observe the past from your present vantage point. You can see patterns you missed then, understand motivations that were unclear, and recognize resources you didn't know you had.

5 When you relive, you become that younger, less experienced version of yourself again, feeling the same powerlessness, confusion, or pain as if it were happening now.

6 If you find yourself reliving rather than remembering, gently bring yourself back to the present. Notice your current surroundings. Feel your feet on the ground. Take deep breaths. Remind yourself of how you have grown since then.

7 You might say to yourself, "That was then, this is now. I was younger then and knew less. I am older now and can respond differently. I survived that experience and learned from it."

8 Practice speaking to your younger self with the compassion you would show a child who was struggling. That past version of you deserves understanding and kindness, not harsh judgment from the more knowledgeable present version.

9 Sometimes it helps to literally speak aloud to your past

self: "You did the best you could with what you knew. You were brave to keep going. I'm proud of how you survived. I'm here now and can take care of things differently."

10 This practice helps heal the split between who you were and who you are, creating integration rather than rejection of your own history.

8

As you transform your relationship with the past, you will discover that what once felt like a prison becomes a foundation, what once felt like a curse becomes a source of wisdom, what once felt like weakness becomes a unique form of strength.

2 The past becomes not something to be escaped but something to be integrated—woven into the tapestry of who you are in a way that adds depth, color, and texture rather than tears and stains.

3 You will find yourself able to speak of difficult experiences without being overwhelmed by them, to remember painful times without being pulled back into pain, to acknowledge harm without being consumed by hatred.

4 This does not mean becoming emotionless about the past. You may still feel sadness for losses, anger at injustices, or grief for what might have been. But these emotions become responses you have rather than states you live in.

5 Others may notice the change in you—how you can listen to their stories of struggle without being triggered, how you can offer perspective without minimizing pain, how you carry yourself with a strength that comes not from avoiding difficulty but from having moved through it.

6 Your past becomes a source of credibility when you offer hope to others facing similar challenges. When you say, "I understand because I've been there too, and I know it's possible to heal and grow," your words carry the weight of lived experience.

7 The reservoir of the past provides not only wisdom but also gratitude. When you see how far you've come, how much you've learned, how you've been able to help others because of what you've been through, even difficult experiences can become sources of unexpected thankfulness.

8 This is the great transformation—from being a victim of your past to being a steward of your experience, from being diminished by what happened to being enlarged by how you responded to what happened.

9 Your past no longer defines your future; instead, your present choices determine how your past will serve your future. The events remain the same, but their power has been redirected from harm to healing, from bondage to freedom, from weakness to strength.

10 Walk forward then with your past as ally rather than enemy, as teacher rather than tormentor, as reservoir rather than cesspool.

11 Let the past inform your wisdom without controlling your choices, contribute to your compassion without hardening your heart, add to your strength without adding to your burdens.

12 For in this way, nothing is truly wasted—not the pain that taught you resilience, not the failure that taught you humility, not the loss that taught you what matters most, not the struggle that taught you your own strength.

13 The past becomes not something to overcome but something to grow through, not something to forget but something to transform, not something to escape but something to redeem through the wisdom and love of the present moment.

22

the Book of Healing

1 Consider the words that have the power to transform both speaker and listener, words that can shift the course of relationships and redirect the flow of pain: "I forgive you."

2 These three simple words carry within them a force more powerful than vengeance, more healing than time, more transformative than justice itself.

3 Yet many people withhold these words, believing that forgiveness is a gift they give to others, not understanding that it is primarily a gift they give to themselves.

4 For when you speak the words "I forgive you," you are not excusing what was done or pretending it didn't matter. You are not saying the harm was acceptable or that consequences should not follow.

5 You are declaring your own freedom from the prison of resentment, announcing your choice to no longer allow another person's actions to control your inner life.

6 In these words lies a profound reclaiming of power—not power over others, but power over your own heart, your own thoughts, your own future.

2 Many believe that forgiveness requires waiting until they feel ready, until the pain has lessened, until the other person has apologized or changed their behavior.

2 They say, "I cannot forgive until I feel differently," not understanding that forgiveness is not a feeling but a decision—a choice to release what cannot be changed.

3 Others believe that forgiveness means forgetting, that to truly forgive they must erase the memory of harm from their minds as if it never occurred.

4 But forgiveness is not amnesia. You can remember what happened while choosing to no longer let it define your present or dictate your future.

5 The wound may leave a scar, and the scar may serve as wisdom, reminding you to choose relationships more carefully or to protect yourself more wisely.

6 Still others believe that forgiveness requires reconciliation, that to forgive means to restore the relationship to exactly what it was before the harm occurred.

7 But forgiveness can exist without reconciliation. You can release your resentment while still choosing not to trust someone who has proven untrustworthy. You can wish someone well while recognizing they are not safe to have close to you.

8 Forgiveness clears your own heart; wisdom determines what kind of relationship, if any, is appropriate moving forward.

3 When you speak the words "I forgive you," whether aloud to the person who harmed you or quietly within your own

heart, you are taking responsibility for your own emotional well-being.

2 You are refusing to remain a victim of circumstances beyond your control, choosing instead to become the author of your own response.

3 This is not about fairness or justice in the larger sense—those may require different actions and different forums. This is about your freedom to live without the constant presence of anger, bitterness, and resentment as your daily companions.

4 These toxic emotions harm the one who carries them far more than they affect their intended target. They are like drinking poison and hoping the other person will feel sick.

5 When you forgive, you stop poisoning yourself with anger that changes nothing about the past but corrodes everything about your present.

6 You take back the power to determine your own emotional state, refusing to let someone else's actions continue to wound you day after day through your own rehearsal of the injury.

7 In this way, forgiveness is an act of self-care disguised as an act of grace toward others.

4 The words "I forgive you" also establish clear boundaries, contrary to what many believe.

2 When you forgive from a place of strength rather than weakness, you are saying, "What you did was wrong, and I will not carry the burden of your wrongdoing in my heart any longer."

3 You are drawing a line between their actions and your reactions, between their choices and your peace, between their behavior and your well-being.

4 This boundary protects you from being controlled by their actions—past, present, or future. Their behavior cannot determine your inner condition because you have chosen to respond rather than react.

5 Forgiveness says, "I am responsible for my own heart, my own choices, my own path forward. You are responsible for yours."

6 This boundary is not a wall but a property line—clear demarcation that allows you to tend your own garden without constantly tending to the weeds someone else has planted.

7 When you know you have the power to forgive, you can engage with difficult people from a place of strength rather than vulnerability, knowing that their actions cannot ultimately control your peace.

5 The act of forgiveness also releases the offender from the debt they owe you—not because the debt wasn't real, but because you choose to stop trying to collect it.

2 This release frees both of you from the ongoing dance of creditor and debtor, victim and perpetrator, wounded and wounding.

3 You stop keeping score, stop waiting for the perfect apology, stop expecting them to somehow make up for what they took from you.

4 This does not mean their actions had no consequences or that justice should not be pursued through appropriate channels. But it means you are no longer personally invested in their punishment as a requirement for your peace.

5 When you release them from the debt, you also release yourself from the exhausting job of trying to collect payment that may never come.

6 You free your mental and emotional energy for more productive purposes than nursing grievances and planning revenge.

7 The release is not for their sake primarily, though they may benefit from it. The release is for your sake, so you can move forward unencumbered by the weight of unpaid debts that were never yours to collect anyway.

6 Speaking the words "I forgive you" is sometimes difficult because we fear it makes us weak, that others will see our forgiveness as permission to harm us again.

2 But true forgiveness comes from strength, not weakness. It takes great courage to choose grace when vengeance feels more satisfying, to choose freedom when holding grudges feels more justified.

3 Weak people cannot truly forgive because they do not have enough sense of self to give up the identity of victim. Strong people can forgive because they know who they are beyond what others have done to them.

4 When you forgive from strength, you make it clear that your choice comes not from inability to defend yourself but from unwillingness to let someone else's actions continue to define your life.

5 Others may indeed mistake your forgiveness for weakness, but their misunderstanding does not change the reality of your strength or the wisdom of your choice.

6 Let them think what they will think. Your forgiveness is not dependent on their understanding any more than your worth is dependent on their approval.

7 You are not forgiving to impress others or to gain their respect. You are forgiving to reclaim your own life from the shadows of past hurts.

7 The words "I forgive you" sometimes need to be spoken to yourself as much as to others.

2 We often carry guilt and shame for our own mistakes, failures, and poor choices, becoming our own harshest judge and most unforgiving creditor.

3 Self-forgiveness requires the same recognition that forgiveness of others requires: that holding onto guilt and shame does not change the past but it does damage the present.

4 When you speak forgiveness to yourself, you are acknowledging your mistakes without allowing them to become your identity, recognizing your failures without letting them define your future.

5 You are taking responsibility for what you did wrong while refusing to take responsibility for being fundamentally flawed or irredeemably damaged.

6 The same power that allows you to release others from their debts to you allows you to release yourself from debts to your own perfectionist expectations.

7 Self-forgiveness does not mean making excuses for harmful behavior or avoiding appropriate consequences. It means treating yourself with the same compassion you would show a friend who had made similar mistakes.

8 For if you cannot forgive yourself, you will struggle to genuinely forgive others, and if you cannot receive forgiveness, you will find it difficult to offer it.

8 Sometimes forgiveness must be offered in stages, like medicine taken in doses appropriate to what the body can handle.

2 You may forgive the fact of what happened before you can forgive the person who did it. You may forgive the person before you can trust them again. You may forgive the action before you can forget its impact.

3 This is not partial forgiveness or incomplete forgiveness —it is human forgiveness, offered by beings with limited capacity who must process hurt the way they process all experiences: gradually, over time.

4 Do not judge yourself for needing to forgive repeatedly, for finding the same resentment arising again even after you thought you had released it.

5 Like weeds in a garden, old hurts sometimes send up new shoots even after you thought you had pulled them up

by the roots. When this happens, simply forgive again.

6 Each act of forgiveness weakens the hold that past hurt has on your present peace, even if it does not eliminate it entirely in a single moment.

7 Be patient with the process as you would be patient with physical healing, understanding that some wounds take longer to heal than others, that healing happens according to its own timeline, not according to your impatience to be finished with pain.

9 The ultimate power in the words "I forgive you" lies not in their effect on the other person but in their effect on the one who speaks them.

2 These words transform the speaker from victim to agent, from prisoner to free person, from someone controlled by past events to someone empowered to shape their own response.

3 In choosing forgiveness, you join the ranks of those who have discovered that the greatest revenge against those who wound you is to refuse to let their wounding control you.

4 You demonstrate that you are larger than what has been done to you, stronger than the circumstances that tried to diminish you, more powerful than the people who attempted to define you by their treatment of you.

5 When you forgive, you step into the fullness of your own agency, claiming the right to determine your own emotional state regardless of others' actions.

6 This is perhaps the most profound form of taking responsibility—not for others' choices, which were never yours to control, but for your own response, which has always been within your power.

7 In the end, forgiveness is not primarily about the past but about the future—not about what was done to you but about what you choose to do with what was done to you.

Here I Am

10 Let the words "I forgive you" become familiar on your tongue, not because you are weak or naive, but because you are strong and wise.

2 Forgive quickly when possible, not because the offense was small, but because you are too valuable to waste your life energy on resentment.

3 Forgive repeatedly when necessary, not because you are foolish, but because freedom is worth fighting for again and again.

4 Forgive completely when you are able, not because you are a saint, but because you are human and humans were not designed to carry the weight of unprocessed anger indefinitely.

5 Speak these words when they need to be heard, whether by others who have wronged you or by yourself when you have fallen short of your own standards.

6 Let forgiveness become not just something you do but part of who you are—not someone who ignores wrong or accepts abuse, but someone who refuses to let others' choices determine their own inner condition.

7 For in learning to forgive, you learn the deepest truth about power: that the greatest strength lies not in the ability to wound others but in the ability to heal yourself.

8 The words "I forgive you" are words of liberation, spoken by the free to claim their freedom, offered by the strong to maintain their strength, declared by the wise to protect their peace.

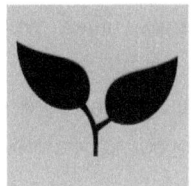

23

the Book of Beginnings

1 Consider the profound truth that echoes through every human heart: the longing for fresh starts, new chances, and the possibility that tomorrow might be different from yesterday.

2 This desire for beginning again is not weakness but wisdom, not failure but hope, not escape but the deepest recognition of what it means to be alive and growing.

3 For we are creatures made for transformation, designed not to remain static but to move through seasons of ending and beginning, death and rebirth, closing and opening.

4 Every sunrise declares the possibility of beginning again. Every spring proclaims that what seemed dead can live. Every breath you take is both an ending and a beginning—releasing what was, receiving what is.

5 Yet many sojourners resist this natural rhythm, clinging to what was, fearing to release what no longer serves, believing that starting over means admitting defeat.

6 They carry their past like heavy chains, their mistakes like permanent tattoos, their failures like sentences of eternal judgment.

7 But listen: the universe itself is in constant motion, constantly beginning. Stars are born from the death of other stars. Forests grow from fallen trees. Rivers carve new channels when old ones are blocked.

8 Nothing in nature remains forever unchanged, and that which has ended contributes to something new beginning.

9 The longing in your heart for a fresh start is not foolish hope but recognition of the deepest pattern of existence itself—that all things move through cycles of completion and commencement.

10 This longing calls you not to deny what has been but to trust what might yet be, not to erase your history but to write new chapters, not to pretend the past didn't happen but to believe the future can be different.

2 New beginnings come to us in many forms and for many reasons, each carrying its own challenges and opportunities.

2 Some beginnings follow failure—when our carefully laid plans crumble, when our relationships end badly, when our careers derail, when our health breaks down, when our financial security disappears.

3 In these moments, beginning again feels less like choice and more like necessity, less like adventure and more like survival.

4 The person who must rebuild after bankruptcy did not choose this beginning, yet it offers possibilities that prosperity never provided—the chance to discover what truly matters, to build more wisely, to value differently.

5 The individual whose marriage has ended faces not just

loss but also the opportunity to discover who they are apart from that relationship, to heal old wounds, to love more authentically next time.

6 The worker whose career has stalled or ended must grieve what they thought their life would be, but they also gain the chance to explore paths they never considered, to develop gifts they never used.

7 Other beginnings follow loss—the death of loved ones, the end of periods of life, the departure of children, the conclusion of roles that gave us identity.

8 These losses create empty spaces that feel overwhelming, but empty spaces are also open spaces, ready for new growth, new relationships, new purposes.

9 The parent whose children have grown and left home grieves the end of daily caregiving but discovers freedom to pursue dreams deferred, to rediscover partnership with their spouse, to explore aspects of themselves that parenting had overshadowed.

10 The retiree who has lost the structure and identity of career faces uncertainty but also gains time for reflection, relationship, and pursuits that work never allowed.

11 Still other beginnings arise from the simple recognition that our current path, while not obviously wrong, no longer fits who we are becoming.

12 These are perhaps the most challenging beginnings because they require us to leave what appears to be working in order to seek what might work better.

13 The successful professional who feels spiritually empty, the secure relationship that has grown stagnant, the comfortable lifestyle that no longer brings joy—these require courage to change not because they are terrible but because they are merely adequate.

14 Yet adequacy is the enemy of authenticity, and

sometimes we must leave good situations to find great ones, familiar paths to discover true ones.

3 Beginning again requires a particular kind of courage—not the courage of those who have never failed, but the courage of those who have failed and choose to try again.

2 This is the courage to be vulnerable after being wounded, to trust after being betrayed, to hope after being disappointed, to love after being rejected.

3 It is the courage to admit that what you built before was not strong enough, that what you believed before was not true enough, that who you were before was not complete enough.

4 Such courage does not come from feeling strong but from choosing strength despite feeling weak, not from certainty but from commitment despite uncertainty.

5 The courage required for new beginnings acknowledges fear without being controlled by it, recognizes risk without being paralyzed by it, accepts the possibility of failure without being prevented by it.

6 This courage grows not from the absence of doubt but from action taken in the presence of doubt, not from knowing the outcome but from trusting the process.

7 Consider the seed that must break open to become a plant. The seed cannot know what kind of tree it will become, cannot see the soil it will grow in, cannot predict the weather it will face.

8 Yet the seed contains within itself the courage to break apart, to trust the darkness, to reach toward light it cannot yet see.

9 So too must you find the courage to break open the shell of who you have been, to trust the uncertain soil of new circumstances, to reach toward possibilities you cannot yet fully envision.

10 This courage is not reckless but wise, not blind but

deeply seeing, not careless but profoundly caring about the potential that lies within current limitations.

11 The courage to begin again says: "I matter enough to grow. My dreams matter enough to pursue. My future matters enough to risk. My authentic self matters enough to discover."

12 Such courage often appears not as bold confidence but as quiet determination, not as dramatic gesture but as small daily choices to move toward something better.

13 The courage to begin is often simply the courage to take the next small step, then the next one, then the next, until you discover you have traveled much farther than you thought possible.

4 Beginning again requires not just moving toward something new but releasing what no longer serves—and this may be the more difficult task of all.

2 We become attached not only to things and people but to identities, beliefs, patterns, and stories about ourselves that may have outlived their usefulness.

3 The identity that served you in youth may constrain you in midlife. The beliefs that comforted you in easier times may burden you in more complex circumstances.

4 The patterns that protected you when you were vulnerable may isolate you when you need connection. The story you told about your limitations may prevent you from discovering new capabilities.

5 To begin authentically, you must inventory what you carry and choose consciously what to keep and what to release.

6 This is not about rejecting your entire past but about distinguishing between what has served its purpose and what continues to serve growth.

7 The snake must shed its skin not because the old skin

was bad but because it no longer fits. The snake that refuses to shed will be constrained, uncomfortable, unable to grow.

8 What identities have you outgrown? What beliefs no longer fit your expanding understanding? What relationships drain more than they nourish? What commitments feel more like obligations than choices?

9 Releasing what no longer serves requires both gratitude and courage—gratitude for how these things once helped you, courage to let them go even when they feel familiar.

10 The graduating student must release the identity of being a learner to become a practitioner. The newly married person must release some independence to gain partnership. The new parent must release certain freedoms to embrace responsibility.

11 Each transition requires this conscious releasing, this grateful goodbye to what was in order to make space for what might be.

12 Sometimes what must be released is not obviously harmful but simply finished—the project that has reached completion, the phase of life that has served its purpose, the version of yourself that was appropriate for earlier circumstances.

13 The difficulty lies not in recognizing what is obviously toxic but in releasing what is merely outdated, not in leaving what hurts but in graduating from what helped.

14 Yet holding onto what has outlived its purpose prevents new growth just as surely as holding onto what is harmful.

15 The gardener who refuses to prune dead branches may think they are preserving the tree, but they actually prevent new growth and weaken the whole plant.

16 Learn to release with blessing rather than bitterness, with appreciation rather than anger, with celebration of what was rather than regret that it must end.

5 One of the most frightening aspects of new beginnings is the period of not-knowing that lies between ending and beginning, between what was and what will be.

2 This liminal space—neither here nor there, neither past nor future—feels uncomfortable because it offers no guarantees, no clear map, no certain destination.

3 Yet this space of not-knowing is not empty wasteland but fertile ground, not barren desert but soil rich with possibility.

4 It is in the uncertainty between identities that new identity can emerge. It is in the gap between roles that authentic self can appear. It is in the pause between chapters that new stories can be conceived.

5 The discomfort of not-knowing is actually the discomfort of growth itself—the stretching that occurs when old containers become too small, the reaching that happens when familiar ground proves insufficient.

6 Consider the butterfly emerging from the chrysalis. During transformation, the caterpillar literally dissolves into soup before reorganizing into something entirely new.

7 There is no moment during this process when the creature is clearly either caterpillar or butterfly—it exists in a state of pure becoming, undefined by what it was or what it will be.

8 This phase of dissolution and reformation cannot be rushed, cannot be controlled, cannot be predicted precisely. It requires trust in the process itself.

9 Similarly, human transformation often requires passages through periods of uncertainty, confusion, and not-knowing that feel like being lost but are actually necessary stages of being found.

10 The person between careers may feel anxious about their undefined status, but this uncertainty creates space to

discover what they truly want to do rather than simply what they know how to do.

11 The individual recovering from loss may feel disoriented by the absence of familiar roles and routines, but this disorientation opens possibility for discovering who they are beyond those definitions.

12 The sojourner questioning old beliefs may feel frightened by the lack of certainty, but this questioning creates room for faith that is chosen rather than inherited, personal rather than borrowed.

13 Learn to see not-knowing not as failure to progress but as necessary preparation for authentic progress, not as being lost but as being open to finding something better than what you were looking for.

14 In the fertile darkness of not-knowing, seeds of possibility are germinating. What feels like emptiness may actually be fullness—fullness of potential waiting for the right conditions to emerge.

15 Trust the process of not-knowing. Rest in the uncertainty. Allow the questions to remain unanswered while new answers form in the depths of your being.

16 For it is often precisely when we stop trying to force clarity that true clarity begins to dawn, when we stop grasping for false certainty that authentic direction begins to emerge.

6 Understanding how endings enable beginnings transforms our relationship with both conclusion and starting, both death and birth.

2 Many people fear endings so much that they prevent necessary beginnings, clinging to the familiar even when it no longer serves, remaining in situations that have outlived their purpose rather than facing the uncertainty of change.

3 But endings are not the opposite of beginnings—they

are beginnings' essential partners, creating the space and energy required for new growth.

4 Consider how nature demonstrates this principle in every season. Autumn's ending creates conditions for spring's beginning. The tree that does not drop its leaves cannot produce new ones. The plant that does not complete its life cycle cannot produce seeds for new growth.

5 Death feeds life. Completion enables beginning. Conclusion creates space for new creation.

6 In human experience, this means that the marriage that ends may enable better relationships to begin. The career that concludes may create space for more authentic work. The belief system that dissolves may allow for deeper faith.

7 Even failure, while painful, often provides what is necessary for eventual success. The business that fails teaches lessons that lead to better business decisions. The relationship that ends badly reveals patterns that can be changed in future relationships.

8 The mistake that causes shame can become the source of humility that enables wisdom. The loss that brings grief can create space for new forms of love.

9 This does not mean that all endings are good or that all pain serves a purpose, but it does mean that even difficult endings can become fertile ground for meaningful beginnings if we learn to work with them rather than simply against them.

10 The art lies in learning to complete things well—to honor what was while creating space for what might be, to grieve losses while remaining open to gains, to acknowledge failures while maintaining hope for future success.

11 Some endings we choose; others are chosen for us. But in either case, we can choose how to relate to the ending—with resistance that prolongs suffering or with acceptance that enables transformation.

12 When you recognize that an ending is necessary or

inevitable, ask not "How can I prevent this?" but "How can I complete this well? What do I need to learn from this experience? What gifts can I carry forward? What burdens can I leave behind?"

13 The person who learns to end well learns to begin well, for they understand that every authentic beginning requires some form of death to what was.

14 This death is not violent destruction but gentle release, not bitter abandonment but grateful graduation, not fearful running but courageous progression.

15 Honor your endings by completing them consciously rather than simply enduring them. Say your goodbyes clearly. Express your gratitude openly. Acknowledge your grief honestly. Take your lessons willingly.

16 In this way, endings become not just conclusions but commencements, not just deaths but births, not just closings but openings to new possibilities.

7 The practical work of beginning again requires both inner preparation and outer action, both changing how you think and changing how you live.

2 Begin within by examining honestly where you are and where you want to go, what has worked and what has not, what you want to keep and what you need to release.

3 This requires the courage to see yourself clearly—not with harsh judgment that paralyzes, but with honest assessment that enables improvement.

4 Ask yourself: What patterns keep repeating in my life that I want to change? What dreams have I deferred that still call to me? What aspects of my current situation drain my energy rather than renewing it?

5 What would I attempt if I knew I could not fail? What would I stop doing if I were not afraid of others' reactions? What would I begin if I trusted my own wisdom?

6 These questions create the foundation for authentic change by connecting you with your own deep knowing about what serves your growth and what hinders it.

7 Then begin to take small, concrete steps toward the new beginning you envision. New beginnings rarely happen all at once but unfold through accumulated choices, daily disciplines, and repeated actions in new directions.

8 The person who wants to change careers might begin by taking evening classes, volunteering in their field of interest, or simply reading about new possibilities.

9 The individual seeking to improve relationships might begin by practicing better listening, expressing appreciation more frequently, or setting healthier boundaries.

10 The seeker wanting to deepen spiritual life might begin with daily meditation, regular reading of wisdom literature, or joining a community of fellow seekers.

11 Remember that beginnings are not about perfection but about direction. You do not need to know exactly where you are going or how you will get there. You need only to know the next right step and be willing to take it.

12 Expect resistance—both from within yourself and from others. Beginning again challenges not only your own comfortable patterns but also others' expectations of who you are and how you should live.

13 Some people may try to discourage your new beginning because it threatens their own reluctance to change, because it challenges their assumptions about what is possible, or because they benefit from keeping you in familiar roles.

14 Do not let others' fear or comfort with your old patterns prevent your growth into new ones. Their resistance often reflects their own fear of change, not wisdom about your situation.

15 Similarly, expect your own internal resistance. Parts of

you will want to return to familiar patterns even when those patterns no longer serve you well.

16 Change feels risky even when staying the same is actually riskier. Growth feels uncertain even when remaining static is actually more dangerous.

17 Be patient with your own process of beginning again. Allow for setbacks without interpreting them as failures. Allow for slow progress without demanding immediate transformation.

18 Some beginnings happen gradually, like dawn breaking slowly across the sky. Others happen suddenly, like lightning illuminating the landscape. Both are valid, both are natural, both can lead to authentic transformation.

8 As you embark on new beginnings, remember that you do not travel alone. Others have walked similar paths before you, and their wisdom can light your way.

2 Seek out mentors who have made transitions similar to yours. Learn from their experiences, their mistakes, their discoveries. Let their stories inspire and guide your own journey.

3 Find companions who are also in seasons of new beginning. Share your struggles and encouragements. Support each other through uncertainty and celebrate each other's progress.

4 Create or join communities that understand the challenges of change and growth. Whether formal groups or informal friendships, these connections provide the support necessary for sustained transformation.

5 Remember too that your new beginning, while personal, can serve others. Your courage to change gives others permission to change. Your willingness to grow inspires others to grow.

6 The parent who returns to school shows their children

that learning never ends. The individual who leaves an unfulfilling job demonstrates that security is not the highest value. The person who ends a harmful relationship models that we deserve to be treated well.

7 Your new beginning becomes part of the larger story of human growth and possibility, contributing to the collective evolution of consciousness and community.

8 In this way, your personal transformation serves not just your own development but the development of all whose lives you touch.

9 As you grow in wisdom, you become someone who can mentor others in their own new beginnings. As you learn to navigate change, you become someone who can guide others through uncertainty.

10 The fruit of successful new beginnings is not just personal fulfillment but increased capacity to serve others who seek similar growth.

9 Not all attempts at new beginnings succeed in the ways we initially envision, and this too is part of the wisdom of growth and change.

2 Sometimes what we thought was a new beginning reveals itself to be preparation for a different beginning altogether. Sometimes our first attempts at change teach us what we really need to change.

3 The job we thought would fulfill us may prove disappointing, but it may also teach us what kind of work actually would fulfill us. The relationship we entered with high hopes may not last, but it may show us how to love and be loved more skillfully.

4 Even failed beginnings serve the larger process of discovering who we are and what we truly want. They are not wasted efforts but necessary experiments in the laboratory of becoming.

5 Learn to see setbacks not as evidence that change is impossible but as information about how to change more effectively.

6 The business that fails teaches lessons about planning, marketing, or management that can be applied to future ventures. The diet that doesn't work reveals insights about motivation, habits, or health that can inform better approaches.

7 Persistence does not mean repeating the same failed approach endlessly but learning from what doesn't work and adjusting strategy accordingly.

8 Sometimes the greatest success comes not from achieving what we originally intended but from becoming the kind of person who could achieve something even better.

9 The journey toward one goal may develop qualities—resilience, courage, wisdom, compassion—that enable pursuit of more meaningful goals than we originally conceived.

10 Trust that even imperfect new beginnings move you forward on the path of growth, even when they don't deliver exactly what you expected.

11 The very act of attempting to change, regardless of immediate success, strengthens your capacity for future change. Each beginning makes subsequent beginnings easier.

12 You develop the muscles of courage, the skills of navigation, the tolerance for uncertainty that all serve future transformation efforts.

10 Remember always that the deepest new beginning available to any sojourner is the daily choice to begin again —not just in dramatic life changes but in moment-to-moment decisions to respond differently than you have before.

2 Every moment offers the possibility of a fresh start. Every breath gives you the chance to breathe more deeply. Every interaction provides opportunity to connect more authentically.

3 Every mistake can be followed by a better choice. Every failure can be succeeded by a wiser attempt. Every ending can become the prelude to a more meaningful beginning.

4 The power to begin again is not reserved for special occasions or major life transitions but is available to you in this very moment, whatever your circumstances.

5 Today you can begin to speak more kindly, think more clearly, love more freely, serve more generously, live more fully.

6 Today you can begin to release old resentments, heal old wounds, forgive old mistakes, pursue old dreams.

7 Today you can begin to become the person you have always sensed you could be but perhaps have never fully allowed yourself to become.

8 This beginning does not require perfect conditions, unlimited resources, or others' permission. It requires only your willingness to choose growth over stagnation, possibility over limitation, hope over fear.

9 The life you have always wanted is not somewhere else, waiting for you to find it. It is here, waiting for you to begin it.

10 The person you have always wanted to become is not someone else entirely but is you, more fully realized, more authentically expressed, more courageously lived.

11 Begin again, fellow sojourner. Begin with this breath, this choice, this moment. Begin with whatever you have, wherever you are, however you can.

12 For in the end, the secret of all new beginnings is simply this: the willingness to begin, again and again and again, until beginning becomes not just something you do but who you are—someone always growing, always becoming, always open to what might be possible.

13 Let every dawn remind you that beginning again is the most natural thing in the world. Let every season show you that transformation is the way of all life.

14 And let your own new beginnings, however small or large, be part of the great renewal that is always happening, always possible, always calling you forward into the fullness of who you were created to be.

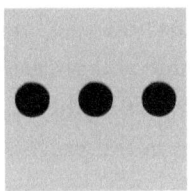

24

the Book of Waiting

1 Consider how much of life is spent in the spaces between —between the decision and its result, between the seed and the harvest, between the question and the answer, between the leaving and the arriving.

2 For every moment of action there are countless moments of waiting, yet few sojourners learn the art of inhabiting these spaces with grace and purpose.

3 Most see waiting as dead time, as interruption to their real life, as obstacle to overcome rather than territory to explore.

4 They fill waiting with distraction, with anxious planning, with restless movement that accomplishes nothing but avoids the discomfort of stillness.

5 But the wise sojourner understands that waiting is not the absence of living but a different kind of living—one that requires its own skills, offers its own gifts, and serves its own essential purposes on the journey.

6 For in the spaces between action, important things happen that cannot happen in any other way: clarity emerges, strength rebuilds, wisdom integrates, and the soul prepares for what comes next.

7 The question is not how to eliminate waiting from your journey—this is impossible and undesirable—but how to wait in ways that serve your growth rather than diminish it.

8 How to be present in the pause without being paralyzed by it, how to remain open to possibility without being consumed by anxiety about outcomes.

2 There is a profound difference between patience and procrastination, though they may appear similar to the casual observer.

2 Procrastination is the avoidance of necessary action, the postponement of what should be done now, the substitution of busywork for real work.

3 It stems from fear—fear of failure, fear of success, fear of judgment, fear of the effort required or the changes that action might bring.

4 The procrastinator waits not because waiting serves any purpose but because acting feels too threatening, too uncertain, too demanding.

5 Patience, by contrast, is the conscious choice to wait when waiting serves a greater purpose than immediate action would serve.

6 It recognizes that some things cannot be rushed, that some outcomes require time to develop, that some opportunities are not yet ready for action.

7 The patient person waits not from fear but from

wisdom, not from avoidance but from understanding of timing and readiness.

8 They wait actively, using the time between action to prepare, to learn, to grow in ability for what lies ahead.

9 Patience trusts the process while procrastination fears it. Patience prepares for action while procrastination avoids it. Patience serves the goal while procrastination serves the ego's need for comfort.

10 The sojourner who learns to distinguish between these two forms of waiting gains power over their own journey, neither rushing prematurely nor delaying unnecessarily.

3 Much suffering comes from the illusion that we control the timing of outcomes, that our desires and plans should determine when things happen in our lives.

2 We plant seeds and demand immediate flowers. We begin relationships and expect instant intimacy. We start new ventures and grow frustrated when success doesn't arrive on our preferred schedule.

3 This impatience stems from forgetting our place in the larger order of things—we are participants in processes much larger than ourselves, subject to rhythms beyond our commanding.

4 The seed knows when conditions are right for sprouting, but the gardener cannot force this knowledge. The body knows its own pace of healing, but the patient cannot rush recovery through willpower alone.

5 Opportunities develop according to their own timeline, not according to our convenience. Other people change and grow at their own pace, not at the speed our relationships would prefer.

6 Even our own readiness develops gradually—we may know intellectually what we want to do but lack the emotional

or spiritual capacity to do it well until more preparation has occurred.

7 The wise sojourner learns to read the signs of readiness in themselves and in their circumstances, waiting for the intersection of preparation and opportunity that creates the right moment for action.

8 They understand that premature action often wastes energy and creates problems that patient waiting would have avoided.

9 But they also recognize that opportunities do pass, that some waiting is simply fear in disguise, that readiness is sometimes a choice rather than a feeling.

10 The art lies in discerning when to wait for better timing and when to act despite imperfect conditions.

4 When life feels stuck, when progress seems impossible, when the same day repeats endlessly without apparent change or growth, the temptation is to conclude that nothing important is happening.

2 But beneath the surface of apparent stagnation, essential processes often unfold that require stillness rather than movement, internal work rather than external activity.

3 Consider how trees appear to do nothing during winter months, standing bare and motionless while life happens elsewhere. Yet in this apparent dormancy, crucial work occurs —roots deepen, strength consolidates, and preparation for spring's growth takes place in ways invisible to observers.

4 So too in human life do periods of apparent stuckness often coincide with important internal development that cannot happen during seasons of intense activity and change.

5 The person recovering from loss may appear to be simply waiting for time to pass, but actually they are doing the deep work of integration, learning to carry their experience in ways that heal rather than harm.

6 The individual between careers may seem unproductive, but they may be discovering aspects of themselves that busy productivity had obscured, clarifying values that will guide better choices ahead.

7 The relationship that feels stuck in familiar patterns may be building the foundation of trust and understanding necessary for deeper intimacy that quick fixes could never create.

8 When you feel stuck, ask not "How do I get out of this as quickly as possible?" but "What is trying to develop in me during this time? What am I learning that I could not learn while moving? What strength am I building that will serve me when movement resumes?"

9 Sometimes the best response to feeling stuck is not increased effort but deeper acceptance of where you are, trusting that this too serves your journey even when you cannot see how.

5 There is profound meaning to be found in the pause between movements, in the silence between notes, in the rest between breaths.

2 Music is not made of notes alone but of the spaces between them. Without rest, melody becomes noise. Without pause, rhythm becomes chaos.

3 So too human life requires intervals of stillness to give shape and meaning to periods of activity.

4 In the pause, you discover what the constant motion hides—what you actually think beneath the noise of others' opinions, what you actually feel beneath the rush of daily demands, what you actually value beneath the pressure of social expectations.

5 In the pause, integration happens. The experiences you have accumulated begin to settle into wisdom. The lessons you have encountered begin to change from information into understanding.

6 In the pause, priorities clarify. What seemed urgent reveals itself as merely immediate. What seemed important reveals itself as merely busy. What actually matters emerges from beneath the clutter of lesser concerns.

7 In the pause, strength rebuilds. The energy depleted by constant doing gradually restores itself. The capacity diminished by continuous output slowly renews through rest and reflection.

8 In the pause, creativity incubates. Ideas that were struggling to form in the midst of activity find space to develop. Solutions that were blocked by effort emerge through relaxation of trying.

9 The person who cannot tolerate pauses, who must fill every silence with sound and every stillness with movement, cuts themselves off from these essential processes.

10 They mistake the pause for emptiness when it is actually fullness—full of potential, full of restoration, full of preparation for what comes next.

6 Learning to wait productively requires developing new skills that our culture of constant activity rarely teaches.

2 Practice presence in the current moment rather than constantly projecting into the future. The waiting time is not just a bridge to somewhere else—it is a place in itself, with its own landscape to explore and gifts to offer.

3 Practice attention to what is actually happening right now rather than to what you wish were happening or fear might happen. Often, important things are occurring in the present that you miss while focused entirely on when and how things will change.

4 Practice curiosity about the process itself. What is this waiting time revealing about your fears, your attachments, your assumptions about how life should unfold? What is it teaching you about patience, about trust, about your relationship with control?

5 Practice gratitude for what the waiting time makes possible. Rest that busy-ness prevented. Reflection that constant motion interrupted. Relationships that rushing through life didn't allow time to nurture.

6 Practice preparation without anxious striving. Use waiting time to develop skills, gather resources, clarify intentions—not frantically but steadily, not desperately but purposefully.

7 Practice trust in processes larger than your personal timeline. Some things genuinely cannot be rushed, and trying to force them often damages what you're hoping to achieve.

8 Practice meaningful activity that doesn't depend on specific outcomes. Read, create, serve others, learn new things—not to make time pass but to live fully even while waiting for other things to develop.

9 The person who masters these practices discovers that waiting becomes not merely tolerable but valuable, not just something to endure but something to inhabit with purpose and grace.

7 Sometimes the waiting we endure is not for something we want but with something we cannot change—illness that must run its course, grief that must be processed, circumstances that must be endured.

2 This form of waiting requires different skills than waiting for positive outcomes. It asks us to find meaning not in anticipation but in endurance, not in hope for change but in acceptance of what cannot be altered.

3 When you must wait with pain rather than for pleasure, with loss rather than for gain, with limitation rather than for opportunity, the temptation is to conclude that such time is wasted, that nothing valuable can emerge from unwanted experience.

4 But even unwelcome waiting can become productive when approached with wisdom rather than mere resignation.

5 Waiting with illness can teach patience with your body's limitations and appreciation for health when it returns. It can deepen empathy for others who suffer and clarify what matters most when energy is limited.

6 Waiting with grief can integrate the reality of loss into your continuing life, allowing love to persist without the presence that carried it. It can expand your capacity for compassion and your understanding of what it means to be human.

7 Waiting with difficult circumstances can develop resilience you didn't know you possessed, reveal strength that comfort never calls forth, and create wisdom that easy times never provide.

8 The key is neither to rush through such experiences nor to be crushed by them, but to let them teach what they have to teach while they last.

9 Ask not "How long must this continue?" but "What can I learn while this continues? How can I grow through this experience rather than just survive it? What can this unwanted waiting develop in me that I could not develop any other way?"

10 Even suffering can become productive when it is met with conscious presence rather than pure resistance, when it is allowed to transform you rather than simply overwhelm you.

8 One of the greatest challenges of waiting is managing the anxiety that naturally arises when outcomes remain uncertain and timing stays beyond your control.

2 The mind, designed to solve problems and plan ahead, becomes agitated when forced to remain in unknowing, when unable to predict or control what comes next.

3 This anxiety often makes waiting more difficult than it needs to be, adding the suffering of worry to whatever natural discomfort the situation already contains.

4 When anxiety about outcomes begins to dominate waiting time, practice returning attention to what you can control in the present moment rather than what you cannot control about the future.

5 You cannot control when opportunities will appear, but you can control how well you prepare for them. You cannot control other people's responses, but you can control the quality of your own character and actions.

6 You cannot control timing, but you can control how you use the time you have. You cannot control outcomes, but you can control the effort and care you bring to whatever is required of you now.

7 Practice breathing deeply when anxiety arises, reminding yourself that this moment—this breath, this heartbeat, this present experience—is the only place where life actually happens.

8 Practice accepting uncertainty as natural rather than fighting it as unacceptable. The future has always been uncertain; your awareness of this fact does not make it more dangerous.

9 Practice trusting that your ability to handle whatever comes is greater than your current capacity to imagine it. You have survived uncertainties before, adapted to changes you didn't expect, found ways through difficulties you couldn't initially see.

10 The anxiety of waiting often proves more painful than whatever you're waiting for actually turns out to be.

9 As you develop skill in waiting, you begin to notice the subtle signs that indicate when waiting time is drawing to a close and action time is approaching.

2 Internal readiness manifests as clarity about what you want to do, energy for taking action, and peace with the possibility of both success and failure.

Here I Am

3 External readiness shows itself through opening doors, appearing opportunities, and alignment of circumstances that previously seemed stuck or blocked.

4 The convergence of internal and external readiness creates what we call the right time—not perfect timing, which rarely exists, but appropriate timing for the action you're prepared to take.

5 Learning to recognize these signs prevents both premature action that wastes energy and excessive delay that misses opportunity.

6 Some people never act because they wait for perfect conditions that never come. Others act constantly because they cannot tolerate the discomfort of waiting for appropriate timing.

7 The wise sojourner develops the sensitivity to feel when preparation is sufficient, when conditions are favorable, when the next step forward is clarified and ready to be taken.

8 This sensitivity comes through practice—through paying attention to the results of actions taken too early and too late, through noticing when things flow and when they feel forced, through learning to trust both internal guidance and external signals.

9 When the time for waiting is ending, you will often feel it as naturally as you feel when it's time to wake up or time to sleep. The pressure to remain still gives way to pressure to move forward.

10 Trust this natural rhythm. Honor both the seasons of waiting and the seasons of action, understanding that each serves essential purposes in the larger cycles of growth and achievement.

10 In the end, learning to wait well is learning to live well, for life itself is largely composed of intervals between the moments we think of as significant.

2 The person who can only find meaning in dramatic events and major achievements misses the majority of life,

which unfolds in the quiet spaces between peaks of activity.

3 The sojourner who masters the art of waiting discovers that these spaces are not empty intervals to be endured but rich territories to be explored, not delays in their real life but essential parts of their complete life.

4 They find in waiting not just preparation for action but its own form of action—the action of growing, of healing, of integrating, of becoming.

5 They learn that some of life's most important work happens not when they are doing but when they are being, not when they are achieving but when they are simply present to what is.

6 The space between breaths is not emptiness but the pause that makes the next breath possible. The silence between words is not absence but the space that gives words their meaning.

7 So too the waiting periods in your life are not voids but essential pauses that make meaningful action possible, not obstacles to your journey but part of the journey itself.

8 When you learn to wait with grace, you discover that you are always exactly where you need to be—not where you want to be, perhaps, but where your growth requires you to be.

9 You find that the present moment, even when it feels like merely a bridge to somewhere else, contains everything necessary for this stage of your development.

10 The art of waiting transforms from something you endure into something you practice, from time lost into time invested, from delay into development.

11 Let your waiting be active rather than passive, conscious rather than unconscious, productive rather than merely patient.

12 For in learning to wait well, you learn to live fully in every season of your journey, finding meaning not only in the destinations you reach but in every step of the path that leads there.

25

the Book of Tomorrow

1 Consider how we relate to the future as we journey through life, how tomorrow stretches before us like an uncharted territory, sometimes bright with possibility, sometimes dark with fear.

2 Many people approach the future with dread, their vision clouded by past disappointments and present fears. They expect tomorrow to repeat yesterday's pain, bringing fresh versions of familiar wounds.

3 "If I was hurt before, I will be hurt again," they reason. "If I failed once, I will fail again. If loss came before, loss will come again." Thus they live in perpetual preparation for disaster, their hearts closed against hope.

4 Others swing to the opposite extreme, treating the

future as a guaranteed promise, a debt that life owes them. They plan with absolute certainty, as if their desires were commands that reality must obey.

5 "I will be successful," they declare. "I will be healthy. I will be happy. My children will thrive. My plans will unfold exactly as I envision." When reality fails to match their expectations, they feel betrayed by life itself.

6 Still others flee from any thought of tomorrow, overwhelmed by its uncertainty. They cannot bear to make plans or nurture hopes, for the unknown feels too vast and threatening to face.

7 But there is a wiser way to relate to what has not yet come—not as predetermined fate to be dreaded, not as guaranteed outcome to be claimed, not as overwhelming uncertainty to be avoided, but as an unguaranteed reservoir of possible moments not yet experienced.

8 The future is neither curse nor promise, neither enemy nor friend.

9 The future is potential—vast, unformed, waiting to be shaped by the choices we make in the present moment.

10 This understanding transforms how we live today, how we prepare for tomorrow, and how we hold both hope and uncertainty in creative tension.

2 Understand this truth: the future does not exist except as possibility.

2 What will happen tomorrow has not yet been determined, not fully by your past, not entirely by your present circumstances, not even by your most careful plans.

3 Each moment that has not yet arrived is like an empty vessel waiting to be filled.

4 The shape of that vessel may be influenced by what has come before, but its contents remain to be determined by countless factors, many beyond prediction or control.

5 This is both the terror and the beauty of tomorrow—it cannot be fully known, fully controlled, or fully guaranteed. Yet within this uncertainty lies infinite possibility for surprise, for growth, for change, for redemption.

6 Those who have known great pain often forget this. They see tomorrow through the lens of yesterday, expecting the future to be a mere repetition of the past. Their anticipation becomes a form of reliving, experiencing future hurt before it has even occurred—if it occurs at all.

7 But yesterday's storm does not guarantee tomorrow's rain. Yesterday's failure does not predetermine tomorrow's outcome. Yesterday's betrayal does not mean tomorrow's relationships are doomed.

8 The future is not bound by the patterns of the past, though it may be influenced by them.

9 Each new day brings the possibility of unexpected kindness, unforeseen opportunities, surprising healing, and redemptive transformation.

10 Similarly, those who demand guarantees from the future misunderstand its nature. No amount of planning, preparing, or positive thinking can convert possibility into certainty.

11 Life makes no promises beyond this moment.

12 Your health may improve or decline. Your relationships may deepen or end. Your plans may succeed or fail. Your hopes may be fulfilled or disappointed. This is not pessimism but realism—an honest acknowledgment of life's fundamental uncertainty.

13 Yet within this uncertainty is tremendous freedom.

14 If the future is not predetermined, then your choices matter.

15 If tomorrow is not guaranteed, then today becomes precious.

16 If outcomes are not certain, then hope becomes both possible and reasonable.

3 When we view the future as a reservoir of possible moments rather than predetermined fate, it changes everything about how we act in the present.

2 We move from anxiety to preparation. Instead of worrying about what might happen, we ready ourselves for various possibilities. We build our strength, develop our skills, deepen our relationships, and expand our resources—not because we know what's coming, but because we want to be ready for whatever comes.

3 We move from rigid planning to flexible intention. We set goals and make plans while holding them lightly, ready to adapt when circumstances change, opportunities arise, or new information emerges.

4 The person who sees the future as fixed becomes brittle when reality deviates from their expectations.

5 The person who sees the future as possible remains flexible, able to bend without breaking when the unexpected occurs.

6 We move from passive waiting to active participation. If the future is shaped by present choices, then every decision matters. Every word spoken, every action taken, every relationship nurtured, every skill developed contributes to shaping what comes next.

7 This is not the exhausting burden of trying to control everything, but the empowering recognition that we are participants in creating tomorrow, not merely victims of whatever befalls us.

8 We move from despair to hope. When the future is seen as merely an extension of past pain, hope dies. But when tomorrow is understood as genuinely open, hope finds room to breathe and grow.

9 Hope is not the naive belief that everything will turn out well, but the mature recognition that things could turn out

differently than they have before, that healing is possible, that change can occur, that redemption remains within reach.

10 We move from isolation to connection. If the future is shaped by our relationships and interactions, then investing in connections with others becomes not just personally fulfilling but practically wise.

11 The kindness we show today may return to us in unexpected ways tomorrow.

12 The bridges we build now may provide passage when we need it most.

13 The love we offer creates a network of care that extends into an uncertain future.

4 With this understanding of the future comes great responsibility. If tomorrow is not fixed, if our choices matter, if we participate in shaping what comes next, then how we live today carries weight beyond the present moment.

2 This responsibility is not a burden but a privilege—the privilege of agency, of influence, of contributing to the unfolding story of our lives and the lives of those around us.

3 Consider the responsibility we have to our future selves.

4 The person you will be tomorrow, next year, in a decade, depends partly on the choices you make today.

5 Will you give your future self the gift of good health through present care of your body?

6 Will you offer the gift of wisdom through present learning and growth?

7 Will you provide the gift of strong relationships through present investment in others?

8 Will you create the gift of financial stability through present prudence?

9 Will you build the gift of skills and knowledge through present effort and practice?

10 Your future self cannot reach back to change what

you do today, but you can reach forward to bless who you will become.

11 Consider also the responsibility we have to others' futures. Our words and actions create ripples that extend far beyond our ability to see or control. The encouragement we offer may inspire someone to persist through difficulty. The opportunity we provide may change the direction of someone's life.

12 The child we mentor, the colleague we support, the stranger we help—these present moments of connection may prove pivotal in shaping their future possibilities.

13 Even small choices carry this weight. The driver who practices patience creates safer roads for everyone. The neighbor who tends their garden contributes to the beauty others will experience. The citizen who votes thoughtfully participates in shaping the community's future.

14 This responsibility extends to future generations. The environment we protect or pollute, the knowledge we preserve or neglect, the institutions we strengthen or weaken, the values we model or abandon—all of these influence the world our children and grandchildren will inherit.

15 We are not responsible for guaranteeing specific outcomes—that lies beyond human power.

16 But, we are responsible for contributing positively to the reservoir of possibilities from which the future will emerge.

5 In the face of an uncertain future, hope becomes not a luxury but a necessity. Yet hope is often misunderstood, confused with wishful thinking or naive optimism.

2 True hope is not the belief that everything will turn out as we wish, but the conviction that our efforts toward good are worthwhile regardless of the outcome.

3 Hope is not certainty about the future, but commitment to positive action in the present.

4 Hope recognizes that while we cannot control all outcomes, we can influence the direction of possibilities. Like planting seeds, we cannot guarantee the harvest, but we can prepare good soil, choose good seeds, and tend them with care.

5 Hope acknowledges that setbacks and disappointments are part of the human experience while maintaining that they are not the whole story.

6 Where there is life, there is potential for change, growth, and unexpected blessing.

7 This hope is grounded not in circumstances but in the fundamental nature of an open future. Because tomorrow is not predetermined, because possibilities remain, because change is constant, hope always has ground to stand on.

8 Even in the darkest situations, hope whispers, "This is not the end of the story. There are chapters yet unwritten. There are possibilities not yet explored. There are moments of grace not yet experienced."

9 Hope does not deny present pain or minimize current challenges. Instead, it places them within the context of an unfolding story that is not yet complete.

10 The diagnosis that seems devastating today may lead to treatment breakthroughs tomorrow. The relationship that appears irreparable may find unexpected healing. The career that seems derailed may redirect toward something better suited to your gifts.

11 Hope recognizes that our vision is limited, our knowledge incomplete, our perspective partial. What seems like ending may be beginning. What appears as defeat may set the stage for victory. What feels like loss may clear the way for something better.

12 This is not false comfort but realistic recognition of how often life surprises us, how frequently the unexpected occurs, how regularly what seemed impossible becomes possible.

6 The present moment becomes the bridge between the reservoir of the past and the reservoir of the future.

2 It is here, in this moment, that possibilities are chosen and potential becomes actual.

3 When we understand the future as unguaranteed possibility rather than predetermined fate, the present moment gains tremendous significance. This is when choices are made, when actions are taken, when the course of tomorrow is influenced.

4 The present is not just a brief pause between past and future, but the creative space where both memory and possibility meet.

5 Here we draw upon the wisdom of experience while reaching toward the hope of what might be.

6 In this moment, you have power. Not the power to control all outcomes, but the power to influence them. Not the power to guarantee success, but the power to increase its likelihood. Not the power to prevent all suffering, but the power to respond to it with courage and grace.

7 The person paralyzed by fear of the future misses the opportunities of the present.

8 The person consumed by regret over the past wastes the potential of the present.

9 But the sojourner who embraces the present as the place where the future is born lives with both peace and purpose.

10 Each present moment offers choices: Will you speak words of encouragement or discouragement? Will you act with kindness or indifference? Will you move toward your goals or away from them? Will you build connections or create divisions?

11 These choices seem small in isolation, but they accumulate like drops of water that eventually fill the reservoir.

12 The future is not shaped by grand gestures alone but by the steady accumulation of moment-by-moment decisions.

13 The discipline you practice today builds the strength you'll need tomorrow. The relationship you nurture now creates the support you may require later. The skill you develop in this moment expands the opportunities available in the next.

14 Living in the present with awareness of the future means neither anxious worry nor careless neglect, but thoughtful engagement. We act with both spontaneity and wisdom, both freedom and responsibility.

15 This is the paradox of present-moment living: by focusing on now, we serve tomorrow. By attending to what is, we influence what will be. By embracing the current reality, we participate in creating future possibilities.

7 As we learn to relate to the future as possibility rather than predetermined fate, we discover that uncertainty need not be the enemy of peace. In fact, it can become its ally.

2 When we stop demanding guarantees from life, we can enjoy the adventure of not knowing exactly what comes next.

3 When we release the need to control all outcomes, we can appreciate the surprise of unexpected gifts.

4 The couple who cannot know for certain that their marriage will last can choose to love fully today. The parent who cannot guarantee their child's future can invest wholeheartedly in their present relationship. The person who cannot ensure their health will continue can gratefully embrace their current vitality.

5 This approach to the future creates a particular kind of freedom—freedom from the anxiety that comes from trying to secure what cannot be secured, freedom from the disappointment that comes from expecting guarantees that life cannot provide.

6 It also creates a particular kind of urgency—not the

frantic urgency of fear, but the purposeful urgency of opportunity. If this moment matters for tomorrow, then this moment deserves our full attention and best effort.

7 We begin to see preparation not as insurance against disaster but as investment in possibility. We exercise not because we know we'll live long lives, but because vitality enhances whatever life we have. We learn not because success is guaranteed, but because knowledge expands our options.

8 We build relationships not because we can ensure they'll last forever, but because connection enriches the time we have together. We pursue dreams not because we can promise they'll come true, but because the pursuit itself brings meaning and growth.

9 This approach leads naturally to gratitude for the present while we have it, rather than taking it for granted while we chase future security.

10 It leads to engagement with current opportunities rather than endless preparation for perfect conditions that may never come.

11 As we embrace this relationship with the future, we find ourselves preparing for the ultimate uncertainty—the fact that our time here is limited, that our future is not endless, that we are participants in a story larger than our individual chapters.

12 This recognition brings both solemnness and joy, both responsibility and freedom. It makes each moment more precious because we know it is not guaranteed to last, and each choice more significant because we understand its power to influence what comes next.

13 We discover that we need not fear the future or demand guarantees from it. We need only show up fully in the present, make the best choices available to us, and trust that our faithful participation in this moment is contribution enough to the reservoir of possibilities that awaits.

14 For in the end, the future will be what it will be, shaped by countless factors beyond our knowledge or control. But our part in that shaping—the love we offer, the wisdom we share, the beauty we create, the justice we pursue, the hope we maintain—this is both our responsibility and our gift to whatever tomorrow may bring.

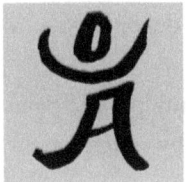

26

the Book of Surrender
(also known as the Book of Todays)

1 Consider how people travel through this world, how they try to direct their steps and plan their path, believing they are captains of their own journey.

2 They plan their routes carefully, they prepare for challenges they expect, they build protection against dangers they foresee, they gather resources for times of need. In these efforts, they find a feeling of security and control.

3 Yet the wise sojourner comes to understand a deep truth: this sense of control is just an illusion, a comforting deception that brings temporary peace but ultimately leads to greater suffering when reality breaks through its fragile walls.

4 For who among you, by thinking hard, can add a single

hour to your life? Who can command the rain to fall or the sun to shine? Who can stop the earth from shaking or the waters from rising? Who can ensure their body stays free from illness or their mind from confusion?

5 Even in matters seemingly within your reach—your daily food, your home, your relationships, your work—your control is partial at best.

6 Economies collapse, opportunities disappear, loved ones leave, health fails, all despite your most careful efforts to prevent such losses.

7 Consider how many people have seen their careful plans undone in moments by circumstances they could neither predict nor prevent.

8 How many have planted crops that drought has dried up or built homes that storms have scattered?

9 How many have saved money that inflation has reduced or built relationships that misunderstanding has broken?

10 The person who believes they are master of their journey walks a path of inevitable disappointment.

11 For the universe operates according to principles and patterns far beyond human control, and even the most powerful among us remains subject to forces they did not create and cannot command.

12 This recognition may at first appear as darkness on the sojourner's path. To acknowledge our fundamental lack of control can seem like surrendering to chaos, accepting helplessness, giving in to forces indifferent to our existence.

2 Many people, confronted with their lack of true control, respond by gripping more tightly what they believe they can master. They multiply their efforts, increase their determination, expand their preparations, and redouble their planning.

2 They create elaborate systems to manage risk, complex strategies to achieve outcomes, detailed schedules to structure time, and rigid rules to govern behavior. In doing so, they hope to carve out a small territory of certainty in an uncertain world.

3 But consider the cost of this pursuit. The person who constantly strives for control lives in perpetual tension, forever fighting against potential threats to their temporary control.

4 Their mind fills with worry about what might go wrong, their body tenses with the effort of maintaining order, their spirit grows weary from endless labor.

5 When events inevitably unfold contrary to their designs, such people experience not merely disappointment but deep distress. For they have staked their security, their identity, and their peace on their ability to determine outcomes. When this ability fails, as it must, they find themselves in crisis.

6 Observe how many illnesses of body, mind, and spirit stem from this futile pursuit of control.

7 How many people suffer from anxious thoughts that disturb their sleep, from tension that shows up as physical pain, from anger that erupts when others fail to follow their expectations, from despair that comes when their best efforts fall short?

8 The person who clutches tightly to the illusion of control finds that what they grasp so desperately becomes a weight too heavy to carry.

9 For they take upon themselves responsibility for outcomes they cannot truly determine, assuming the role of a creator rather than a created being.

10 This weight was never meant for human shoulders to carry. We were not designed to be rulers over our journey but to walk in harmony with forces greater than ourselves.

11 The pursuit of mastery leads not to freedom but to bondage, not to peace but to anxiety, not to joy but to fear.

3 Consider the river as it flows from mountain to sea. It does not struggle against gravity but surrenders to it. It does not fight the shape of the land but adapts to it. It does not resist obstacles but flows around them. In this surrender, it finds its strength and fulfills its purpose.

2 The river does not worry about its destination or fret about its speed. It simply flows according to its nature, responding to the realities it encounters moment by moment. Yet in this seeming passivity, it accomplishes remarkable things—carving canyons, nourishing ecosystems, and ultimately reaching the vast ocean.

3 The wise sojourner learns from the river, understanding that true power comes not from imposing one's will upon the world but from aligning oneself with the greater currents of existence. Not from rigid resistance but from flexible response. Not from anxious striving but from present attention.

4 This wisdom recognizes that while we cannot control external events, we can choose how to meet those events.

5 While we cannot determine what challenges arise on our path, we can decide how to respond to those challenges.

6 While we cannot command the weather of circumstance, we can adjust our sails to work with whatever winds blow.

7 Such wisdom is not fatalism or resignation.

8 The river does not simply lie still and accept whatever happens. It moves with purpose, it adapts with intelligence, it persists with determination.

9 But it does so by working with reality rather than against it, by accepting what is rather than exhausting itself fighting what cannot be changed.

10 In this way, the sojourner discovers a paradoxical truth: surrender leads to greater effectiveness than control.

11 By letting go of the exhausting effort to manage

outcomes beyond their power, they free their energy for creative response to what actually emerges.

12 By accepting reality as it presents itself, they gain the clarity to work skillfully with its patterns rather than uselessly against them.

13 The wisdom of the river teaches that there is a flow to the universe, a current that moves all things toward their fulfillment.

14 The person who learns to sense this current and move with it rather than against it discovers both peace and power that those who struggle for control never know.

4 What appears at first as a sad recognition—that we lack ultimate control—gradually reveals itself as a pathway to profound joy.

2 For in this acknowledgment, the sojourner is freed from burdens never meant for them to carry and invited into a relationship of trust with the Creator and the creation.

3 Consider how a child experiences the world. They do not worry about providing their own food or securing their own shelter. They do not anxiously plan for all possibilities or strive to prevent all possible harms. They simply trust that their needs will be met by those who care for them, and in this trust, they find freedom to fully engage with life as it unfolds.

4 The person who accepts their lack of control recovers something of this childlike trust.

5 Not childish irresponsibility that neglects what is within their proper care, but childlike recognition that they are not and need not be the final authority or provider in their own life.

6 In this recognition comes joy—the joy of release from impossible expectations, the joy of rest from constant effort, the joy of acceptance that replaces anxious resistance, the joy of wonder in exchange for worried calculation.

7 For the person who surrenders the illusion of control

discovers that the universe is not an enemy to be subdued or a chaos to be ordered, but a mystery to be engaged, a gift to be received, a dance to be joined.

8 They find themselves not diminished but expanded by acknowledging their place in the greater whole.

9 The joy of surrender shows up in surprising ways. The sojourner becomes more flexible when plans change, more curious when the unexpected occurs, more present to each moment rather than constantly projecting into an imagined future or replaying a remembered past.

10 They discover deeper connections with others, no longer relating to them primarily as helps or hindrances to their own agenda but as fellow sojourners with whom to share the journey. They experience heightened appreciation for beauty, no longer seeing the world merely as a resource to be managed but as a wonder to be witnessed.

11 Even in times of difficulty, the person who has embraced surrender finds a quiet joy beneath their suffering—not because the suffering itself is good, but because they trust that even this experience, unwelcome though it may be, unfolds within a larger pattern of meaning they may not currently see but can nonetheless trust.

5 As we travel this path of surrender, we gradually adopt a new attitude toward life—not the stance of the controller who seeks to direct all things according to their will, but the posture of one who makes themselves available to whatever each moment brings.

2 This availability is expressed in the simple statement that has echoed through the ages whenever humans have encountered the divine: "Here I am." These words, spoken by prophets and patriarchs, by ordinary people in extraordinary moments, contain the essence of the surrendered life.

3 "Here I am" acknowledges presence—full presence in

this moment, this place, this circumstance, without evasion or distraction.

4 It accepts what is rather than wishing for what might be.

5 It grounds us in current reality rather than fantasy or fear.

6 "Here I am" offers availability—openness to what comes next, willingness to respond, readiness to engage.

7 It does not dictate the terms of engagement but remains receptive to the call of the moment, the needs of others, the guidance of the Spirit of life.

8 "Here I am" expresses trust—confidence that one need not hide or pretend, that one can stand revealed in both strength and weakness, that one's true self is sufficient for what is required. It sets aside the masks and armor that the controlling self uses to manage impressions and outcomes.

9 "Here I am" embodies courage—the courage to be seen as one truly is, to face what truly comes, to respond with what one truly has.

10 It does not guarantee success or safety but offers authentic presence regardless of results.

11 The person who learns to live from this attitude of availability discovers that control, so desperately sought, matters far less than they imagined.

12 For what makes life meaningful is not mastery of circumstances but meaningful engagement with them. Not the absence of difficulty but the fullness of presence within both joy and sorrow.

6 How then shall we live in light of these truths? How shall we walk the path of holy surrender day by day?

2 Practice present attention. The controlling mind constantly projects into the future or dwells in the past, planning what might happen or rehashing what has occurred.

3 The surrendered mind returns again and again to this

moment, this breath, this step on the path, for it is only here that life is actually lived.

4 Practice flexible response. The controlling approach decides in advance how things should unfold and resists when reality diverges from these expectations.

5 The surrendered approach remains open to what actually emerges and adapts creatively to it, finding opportunities even in unwelcome developments.

6 Practice grateful reception. The controlling stance sees the world primarily in terms of how it serves or thwarts one's aims.

7 The surrendered stance receives all experience as a gift—sometimes welcome, sometimes challenging, but always offering something of value when approached with openness.

8 Practice faithful action. Surrender does not mean passive inaction but faithful response.

9 We still act according to our values, talents, and understanding, but without attachment to specific outcomes.

10 We plant seeds but trust the growing to forces beyond ourselves.

11 Practice compassionate presence. The controlling position creates separation—self versus other, ally versus obstacle.

12 The surrendered position recognizes relationships—that we journey together, that others' welfare affects our own, that compassion serves the whole.

13 Practice humble learning. The controlling mind believes it knows what should happen and how things should be.

14 The surrendered mind remains perpetually open to new understanding, willing to be surprised, ready to revise its views in light of emerging reality.

15 Practice trusting release. At the end of each day, consciously release what you cannot control—outcomes,

others' responses, future circumstances—into the care of the Creator. Do what you can with integrity and leave the rest to greater wisdom.

7 Throughout our journey come moments that test our surrender most deeply—times of great loss, serious illness, profound disappointment, or approaching death. In these crucible experiences, the illusion of control becomes most painfully apparent.

2 Even the most carefully tended body eventually fails.

3 Even the most diligently protected relationships sometimes end.

4 Even the most prudently managed resources can suddenly vanish.

5 Even the most meticulously constructed identity must ultimately be relinquished.

6 These moments reveal the fundamental truth that we have never truly been in control. We have been participants in a journey whose ultimate direction and destination remain mysterious, whose full meaning exceeds our comprehension.

7 Yet these same moments offer us our deepest opportunity for surrender—not as defeat but as a homecoming, not as failure but as fulfillment.

8 For in releasing the closed, tight, desperate grip on what cannot be held, we open our hands to receive what has always been offered.

9 The final surrender is not a yielding to meaninglessness but an opening to greater meaning. Not a resignation to purposelessness but a trust in purpose that transcends personal design. Not an abandonment of hope but a hope anchored beyond what we can see.

10 In this surrender, we discover what mystics and sages across traditions have testified: that at the heart of reality lies not cold indifference but warm embrace, not chaotic

meaninglessness but profound intelligence, not hostile force but loving presence.

11 This is the paradox at the heart of our journey: only in acknowledging that we control very little do we discover that we need control very little.

12 Only in recognizing our smallness do we glimpse our participation in greatness.

13 Only in accepting our limitations do we open to the unlimited.

14 The universe, vast and mysterious as it is, does not ask us to be in control, to have all the answers, to prevent all difficulties, or to determine all outcomes. It asks only for our presence, our attention, our participation, our trust.

15 The sojourner, plagued with existential questions - What happens after death? Who am I? What is the meaning of life? - raising the quiet voices to a scream, "Damn the dark, damn the light, damn the lies, damn the truth, damn death and damn life," succumbs to the only question which really matters.

16 But even then, the sojourner understands the question will only be answered from moment to moment.

17 So the sojourner breaks and asks the ultimate selfish question. The only question that truly satisfies the soul. Not the question of what happens after death. Not why am I here. But, the question we yearn for, we live for an answer- "What is going to become of me?"

18 In that moment of utterance the sojourner realizes that they have nothing to offer, no control, no real knowledge. Nothing.

19 And so the sojourner, having journeyed far, stands at last with open hands to the heavens and open heart to the universe, offering the only utterance that has ever been truly possible, the only response required -

20 "Here I am."

Epilogue

In the midst of life and death,
In the quiet space between each breath,
In the midst of light and darkness found,
Where certainty and confusion both abound,
Here I am.
I am neither wise nor ignorant,
My knowledge flows, then turns stagnant.
Neither certain nor completely lost,
A sojourner counting neither gain nor cost,
Neither rich in gold nor poor in spirit,
Owning nothing the world would inherit,
Here I am.

Here I Am

I am not special by the world's measure,
I am not ordinary despite my common treasure.
I am not strong when trials appear,
I am not weak though I tremble with fear.
I am simply that I am,
A brief note in creation's plan,
Here I am.
Between joy that soars and grief that drowns,
Between moments that uplift and days that ground,
Between the mountaintop and valley low,
Between the certainty and the unknown,
Here I am.
Not claiming wisdom beyond my years,
Not hiding from my deepest fears.
Not grasping tightly what will fade,
Not building kingdoms in the shade.
Just standing present, fully aware,
Offering all that I am and all I bear,
Here I am.
In the pendulum swing of happiness and pain,
In the ebb and flow of loss and gain,
In the space between what was and will be,
In this present moment, finally free,
I surrender to the mystery,
Of all I cannot know or see.
Here I am.
Neither striving to become,
Nor regretting what is done.
Neither yearning for tomorrow,
Nor dwelling in past sorrow.
Simply present, wholly true,
Offering what I am to You.

Here I am.

About the Author

David L. Campbell, PhD is a philosopher, educator, and former executive leader whose life was fundamentally altered by a near-death experience that reframed his understanding of human existence. Born and raised in Mississippi—the literary home of William Faulkner, Eudora Welty, and John Grisham—Campbell has spent decades in contemplative study of philosophy, cognitive psychology, theology, and religion, searching for deeper meaning and purpose in the human journey.

Campbell's professional career spans executive leadership and mentorship roles in community colleges across Florida and Mississippi, where he guided institutions and individuals through transformative change. He is the author of self-published Without Fanfare: Creating an Autonomous Followership, which explores leadership dynamics and human agency.

Following his near-death experience, Campbell began urgently reframing a lifetime of journal entries through his radically shifted perspective on mortality and meaning. This intensive philosophical excavation became Here I Am: a Sojourner's bible—a collection of wisdom literature that approaches fundamental human experiences from the transformative angle of understanding ourselves as temporary travelers rather than permanent residents.

Campbell's work emerges from the intersection of lived experience and scholarly inquiry, offering what he describes as "an antidote to both transactional religion and hedonistic nihilism." His writing carries the contemplative depth of the Southern literary tradition while addressing universal questions of meaning, mortality, and authentic living that resonate across cultural and religious boundaries.

Campbell continues to write and reflect from his home in Mississippi, where the rhythms of the South inform his ongoing exploration of what it means to live fully while passing through.

Connect with me online: http://www.10MileMark.com

www.ingramcontent.com/pod-product-compliance
Lightning Source LLC
Chambersburg PA
CBHW021146060526
44107CB00146B/1333/J